advance praise for
UNCORKING MIRACLES

With this fascinating memoir, Rob Bundschu gives us an inspiring record of his spiritual journey that reminds me a lot of my own. The form of his story is different but the content is the same: a transformation from separation to oneness. I highly recommend this book to anyone who wants to see how you can "stumble" onto a path that takes you home, even though there are no accidents along the way. — GARY R. RENARD, the best-selling author of *The Disappearance of the Universe* trilogy and *The Lifetimes When Jesus and Buddha Knew Each Other: A History of Mighty Companions*

When I first met Rob Bundschu, it was around the campfire, and I found a deep thinker, and a person that feels deeply. We were by ourselves because the depth of our conversation might have been a little too much for others. Now you have at your availability the delight I had when I first met Rob Bundschu. — BRUCE H. RECTOR, Co-Owner with his bride Krassimira of *Ahh Winery*; Noted Diner and Bon Vivant; author of *Wine Through Another Glass In the Vineyard, In the Cellar, at the Table — Seven Principles of Practice with the Seen and Unseen Worlds*.

Jacob Gundlach (1816-1894) kept a diary recording daily happenings as he emigrated on various sailing ships from Germany to California. Sadie Towle Bundschu (1886-1947) kept a series of diaries describing her life on Rhinefarm located here in Sonoma Valley. They described her years from 1902 through 1941. Jacob and Sadie's diaries provide rich recounting of their historical experiences. What a treat to read in their own handwriting things they saw and did. Yet as cherished as these writings are they do leave a reader wanting more: What were they thinking, why did they do what they did? They seldom addressed anything more than what they did that day.

Rob Bundschu (1970-?) has answered the family call to record his life's experiences not in diary format, but in this memoir. In so doing he has the space to relate not only his experiences, some of which have been quite challenging, but also his thoughts, his picturesque recollection of inner feelings, and the 'whys' he is who he is. — Adios, JIM BUNDSCHU

Rob takes readers on a truly inspiring journey with his story of overcoming addiction and living a true Miracle. His resilience will leave you feeling that you CAN overcome anything and that you are not alone. *Uncorking Miracles* is a page-turner and an excellent representation of living *A Course in Miracles*. This book will definitely give you a buzz — one that's even better than having a drink! — MARIA FELIPE, author of best-selling book *Live Your Happy*, ACIM international speaker and counselor

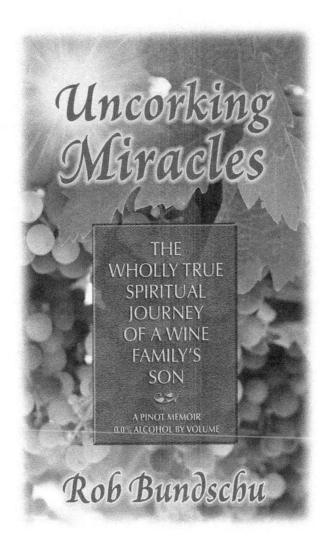

Uncorking Miracles

THE WHOLLY TRUE SPIRITUAL JOURNEY OF A WINE FAMILY'S SON

A PINOT MEMOIR
0.0% ALCOHOL BY VOLUME

Rob Bundschu

LOVALL
VALLEY ROAD

SONOMA CA

UNCORKING MIRACLES:
The Wholly True Spiritual Journey of a Wine Family's Son

by Robert Bundschu

Published by **Lovall Valley Road**

Contact:
lovallvalleyroad@gmail.com

All Course quotes are from *A Course in Miracles*,
copyright ©1992, 1999, 2007 by the Foundation for Inner Peace,
448 Ignacio Blvd., #306, Novato, CA 94949, *www.acim.org*
and *info@acim.org*, used with permission.

ISBN: 978-0-9909750-4-5
Library of Congress Control Number: 2021916698

FRONT COVER PHOTO, DESIGN & TYPOGRAPHY:

D. Patrick Miller / Fearless Literary
www.fearlessbooks.com

BACK COVER PHOTO:
Rob Bundschu

AUTHOR PHOTO:
Sarah Lane

References from the Combined 3rd Edition of *A Course in Miracles*
are signified as follows:
    T-# = Text + Chapter Number
    Roman numerals = Section
    First Number = Paragraph
    Second Number(s) = sentence(s)
    W = Workbook
    pII = Part 2

CONTENTS

*You **are** the Kingdom of Heaven,*
but you have let the belief in darkness enter your mind
and so you need a new light.

—A Course in Miracles T-5.II.4:1

FOREWORD

M Y FAVORITE part of this honest, simply told, and engaging life story by my friend Rob Bundschu is his recollection of seeking, during one dissolute phase of his life, the 'P4BB': the Perfect 4-Beer Buzz. There could be no better metaphor for what depth psychologist Carl Jung described as the unconscious objective of alcoholism: "the equivalent, on a low level, of the spiritual thirst of our being for wholeness." William James likewise suggested that "... drunken consciousness is one bit of the mystic consciousness, and our total opinion of it must find its place in our opinion of that larger whole."

Rob's riotous and sometimes hallucinatory search for a mystic consciousness eventually led him to the modern spiritual discipline known as *A Course in Miracles* (ACIM), which has been described as "graduate school" or the "13ᵀᴴ Step" for followers of the addiction recovery method known as the Twelve Steps of Alcoholics Anonymous. I've written widely about the Course and met Rob, in fact, while waiting in line for dinner at a Course conference some years ago.

While it's not unusual to meet recovering alcoholics in the ranks of ACIM students, what was distinctive about Rob was his sixth-generation membership in a family that runs the legendary Gundlach-Bundschu Winery in Sonoma, California. As his early yearning for the P4BB reveals, Rob did not depend solely on "Gun Bun" vintages for his experiences of low-level mysticism. But at least his roots were sunk deep in the same soil as some of the best fermented spirits available.

In one of its most poignant passages, *A Course in Miracles* powerfully suggests that all of us have a mystical yearning within:

> *This world you seem to live in is not home to you. And somewhere in your mind you know that this is true. A memory of home keeps haunting you, as if there were a place that called you to return, although you do not recognize the voice, nor what it is the voice reminds you of. Yet still you feel an alien here, from somewhere all unknown....*

Our real "home" that the Course speaks of is not some otherworldly realm, but instead the constant inhabitation of what James called our larger "mystic consciousness." Although alcoholics and other addicts are variously perceived as victims of a constitutional illness, a bad upbringing, or their own moral failings, another way to see them is simply as the kind of people who are especially homesick. Regardless of their worldly circumstances, they cannot help but venture out of their ordinary consciousness in search of a more fulfilling realm of self-awareness. Along the way their misadventures may be, like Rob's, quite perilous.

As a publishing professional constantly awash in manuscripts and print production, I seldom have time to endorse books. And I wouldn't ordinarily foreword one which I've helped facilitate (in this case on the production end, not editorially). But after reviewing Rob's journey through the world of spirits of every variety, in this case I just couldn't resist.

Besides, he's my Pinot Noir connection.

— **D. PATRICK MILLER,** author of ***Understanding A Course in Miracles***: *The History, Message, and Legacy of a Profound Spiritual Path* (2ND Edition, Fearless Books, 2021)

PROLOGUE

O DDLY ENOUGH, it happened at the Deuce. Coulda been a Tuesday or a Saturday afternoon, there's not much of a difference when you're unemployed and living off a large inheritance you did nothing to earn. My friend Adrian took the afternoon off from work—if it was a Tuesday—and we were down at our favorite watering hole, The 2AM Club, or "the Deuce" as locals call it, doing what we both love to do most: drinking, smoking and shooting some pool. It was here on this seemingly random, unnamed day that my life took a subtle, yet profound turn.

The Deuce is a bar of some renown. I once read an article—maybe in the *San Francisco Chronicle*—that listed the Deuce as one of the great dive bars in the Bay Area. Along with being a place where local Mill Valley college kids come to hang out during holiday breaks and local drunks come to get their fill (me), the Deuce is also known to have some notable personalities drop by from time to time. For instance, Adrian once shot pool next to Sean Penn. Anyway, Adrian and I were down at the Deuce, once again, when I had my epiphany.

I'd spent many years drinking many beers. Knowing I come from a wine-making family, some people assumed wine was my drink of choice, but for me and my pals, beer was the staple. I did drink wine when the occasion called for it—a nice dinner, or a time or two when we couldn't get beer, and some unlabeled bottles of Pinot or Cab had to be lifted from our winery's party supply. And there was also the occasional time or five when we got liquored up as well.

The point is, I drank. A lot. My drinking, which began when I was about fifteen, grew worse and worse as the years piled up. By the time I hit thirty, the age I was on this fateful day, I had experienced many alcohol-related trials and tribulations, one in particular being an otherworldly, unspeakably dark event I called "The Plunge."

Inevitably, I drank until the point where I would eventually grow apart from my family and most of my friends and isolate — like many alcoholics tend to do. I had no idea that I had a drinking problem, though—that is, not until this day at the Deuce, when I finally got a clue.

We'd only been at the bar for a little bit. I was on my first or second beer. Adrian was shooting pool while I stood and watched, waiting my turn. After a while, I got bored, so I took a short stroll over to the back of the bar, where there was a gaming area tucked into a dark corner. There was an old pinball machine and a couple of video games. I stepped into the small space and just stood there, sipping my beer, gazing at the gaming machines I had played so often in my youth.

After a moment, I turned around and absentmind-edly surveyed the scene, looking at the long, well-worn wooden bar running the length of the room to my right, Adrian and the other guy lining up shots in front of me, and the front door off in the distance, open, letting in a bit of light. It was then, at that moment, seemingly out of nowhere, that I had my realization. The thought was so simple, and yet so deeply profound, that it just stopped me in my tracks. *I'm not having any fun.*

Now this wasn't just about how I was feeling at that moment. In this rare, and I mean *rare*, lucid moment, I realized that drinking in general had lost its shine. It dawned on my barely present, beleaguered and alcohol-soaked mind that I had not had any real fun, or a sense of joy, in a long, long time. I realized my drinking was no longer the blast it had been in my early twenties. Now it was just a habit—it just helped me get by.

I then asked myself, *When's the last time you've had a genuine laugh? One full of joy from the heart, from your gut?* And I couldn't remember. I was awakening to the fact that I'd been in an alcohol-induced fog for as long as I could remember. Could *not* remember.

I believe this simple insight, a subtle shift in the mind, really, initiated the complete life-altering events that were to come —including the scene with Lynette that oc-curred about a week later. As it turns out, my epiphany was a two-parter.

Did I toss my beer in the trash after my moment of clarity and tell Adrian I've seen the light? Ah, no. I kept drinking that day, and onward for the next few days.

There was good reason. My life sucked. I had watched from afar as many of my friends started their careers, got married, and seemed well on their way. I, on the other hand, was still single and stagnating aimlessly in the little town of Mill Valley, a limousine liberal enclave just north of San Francisco over the Golden Gate Bridge (and, I would learn years later, first home of the publisher of *A Course in Miracles!*).

My self-esteem had been deteriorating at about the same rate my drinking had been increasing, bringing me to a point so low that I did not consider myself to be either employable or dateable. I was so down towards the end (of my drinking days), in fact, that one day I told Adrian, "I would never date a woman who would choose *me* as her boyfriend" — thanks, Groucho Marx. It was bad.

By the end of that week, I had all but forgotten about my epiphany and was back to my wayward ways. Yet it must have planted a seed, because I soon decided I was going to make my last stand.

It was early October of 2000 when I woke up one morning, about a week after the epiphany, at the crack of eleven, with an unusually massive hangover. I was in a particularly thick fog and had no clue why. I vaguely remembered that the night before the Giants had beaten the Mets in the first playoff game of the Division Series (and would go on to lose the next three in a row, shattering my dreams of World Series glory), and that I had strolled, or rather staggered, alone from my apartment, where I'd been watching the game, down to the local restaurant/ bar around the corner, where I planned to celebrate the victory and keep the party going. I could remember arriving and sitting down at the bar and ordering a glass of white wine, and then... nothing. I didn't think much of it, though, in my haze, and put the whole night behind me.

I rolled out of bed and thought, "Hmm. What am I gonna do today?"

Then, for no good reason at all, I decided today I was finally going to ask Lynette out. Lynette was a local bartender and server whom I'd had a crush on for several months. I had watched her from afar, like a stalker, but had never had the courage to talk to her, at least beyond ordering a drink. She was the opposite of me in every way: pretty, friendly, positive and vibrant. I, on the other hand, was completely out of shape (at one point, Adrian, who was also my roommate, held up a pair of my jeans and chuckled, "You could use these as a parachute!"), chain-smoking a pack a day to supplement my five-to-ten-beers-a-day habit, and virtually dead on the inside. I was terrified of her. Yet I decided that today I would make my last stand and ask her out. I don't know where the courage came from. There was a kind of a finality about it, a resignation, like if this move didn't work out, I would sail right over the edge of the world and disappear forever.

I waited for a few hours, then took a shower and dressed up as well as I could. Somehow I knew it was

Lynette's birthday today, but I couldn't remember where I came about this information.

The plan was as follows: grab a bottle of Gundlach Bundschu wine, head down to the bar where I hoped she was working, hand it to her, wish her happy birthday, then ask her out. The bottle of wine was the key part of this plan, because it happened to have my last name on it. Being from a wine family was, in my estimation, the only redeemable quality I had left — my last bullet, so to speak. So by God, I was gonna use it.

Still hungover and a little lightheaded, I set off down the street, bottle in hand, with an attitude of *no looking back*. It was only about a five-minute walk from the front door of our apartment down to the fine Italian restaurant. When I arrived, I was surprised to see the narrow bar area, adjacent to the dining area, was quite crowded, about three people deep. Standing in the back of the crowd, near the front door, I nervously scanned behind the bar, half-hoping she wouldn't be there. But oh crap, there she was.

I stood there, staring at Lynette, not sure what to do, when she suddenly turned in my direction, spotted me through the crowd, and looked me straight in the eye. And then to my utter astonishment, her eyes lit up with recognition (of me?), she smiled and then gestured for me to meet her down at the far end of the bar. To say I was shocked is the understatement of the century. The girl of my dreams was acknowledging me! I had *no* idea what this was about.

Keep in mind, to my recollection I had never spoken to her before. But here she was, waving me over. With a huge surge of adrenaline, hope and terror, I began to work my way over to where she was pointing. At this point, I should probably mention that this bar was the very bar I came to the previous night to celebrate the Giants' victory.

After weaving my way through the crowd towards Lynette, she stepped out from under the bar and came right up to me. Shouting above the din, she exclaimed, "Oh my God, how are you? I just wanted to let you know that I hope you're not upset about last night, that I had to ask you to leave..."

At this point, I lost track of what she was saying, as I seemed to lose my ability to hear. It was like a scene in a movie where everyone but the main character fades out of focus and into the background. I literally froze—body, mind and spirit, petrified—in a state of complete and utter humiliation.

Trying to figure out what she was talking about, I quickly reviewed the night before in my mind, but found that there was nothing there. It was blank. I had apparently blacked out the whole night. Yet it was painfully clear that during the blackout I had somehow made a total ass of myself. And here was this lovely woman, kindly attempting to make amends and apologize to me for what I'd done. It was at this moment, in the center of my nightmare, that the following thought streamed through my mind: *You will never date Lynette or any woman like her in the condition you're in.* It was crystal clear, and I knew through and through that it was true.

Meanwhile, Lynette noticed that I had drifted off into a weird comatose state, and she waved her hand in front of my face. "Hello! … Are you listening?"

Suddenly, I snapped out of it. In one swift move, I handed her the bottle of wine and mumbled, "Here, I brought this for your birthday…" Then I turned around, pushed my way through the crowd and out the front door.

A surge of anger rose through me as I marched up the street towards my apartment. *Enough!* I screamed in my mind. *I've had it! I can't take it anymore. I'm done.*

Steaming up the street, I was completely unaware that at that moment, as I berated myself about what I'd just experienced, I was at a critical juncture of my life. I had no clue that I was having my *"There must be another way"* moment.

I would learn years later that there is an instant in a person's life, often after suffering through a difficult situation or circumstance, when the mind and heart finally open enough that the person becomes accessible for learning. From that moment, they are now ready to move on, or shift, to a greater understanding, and their willingness to endure whatever it takes to develop is very strong. I've read several stories of other *"There must be another way"* moments since then, and I can see that bombing with Lynette was mine.

I believe this event with Lynette marked the completion of the epiphany that had started the week before at the Deuce. My soul was *done* with littleness, loneliness and suffering. I was ready to begin what would become an astonishing and completely unexpected spiritual journey that would carry on for the next twenty years, all the way to this moment, as I type these words.

At the time I was stomping up that street, I didn't have a "spiritual" bone in my body—would not have even known what the hell you were talking about. But that, apparently, was about to change…

ONE

A Big Warm Smile

CONTRARY to what some who have met me at the winery seemed to believe, I didn't come out of the chute with a glass of Pinot in my little infant hand. In fact, I was bottle fed, so I didn't even get any Pinot indirectly through my mother. No, I was just a little baby who came into the world, downing milk and chomping Gerber's like everyone else. I was, I guess, raised normally.

But there was one rather unusual event that occurred just a few moments after I was born, one which my mom, Janis Cannon Bundschu, swears to this day happened exactly as she relates it. As she held me in her arms, I turned in her lap, looked her squarely in the eye, and gave her a big warm smile. Now, she knew (because people told her) that newborns weren't capable of such focus, much less a real smile. Nevertheless, she swears I did it. Big, focused, warm smile, from my little infant face. And so this is how I seemingly entered the world.

Whether it's true or not—of course I like to believe it is—the smile wouldn't last long. The world I'd been born into was getting ready to hand me my rear end—in a big

way, though that would come a little later. In the mean-
time, I grew up a pretty lucky kid.

TWO

❧

The Cannons
(Mom's Side of the Family)

I'M THE product of a lineage, and the people in my family affected my life considerably. So probably the best thing to do is to begin with them, just to fill in the background that preceded and led up to my life.

On my mother's side, my grandparents were Robert "Bob" and Betty Cannon. They both grew up in the Los Angeles area in the 1920s and '30s and lived through the Great Depression. Betty Bennett, a beautiful, petite young woman, was an aspiring journalist when she met my grandfather Bob, a six-foot-two, dashing young man with a deep, John Wayne-like baritone voice and a particular confidence and charm.

As the story goes, my grandma had a choice to date a firefighter with good job security—no small thing in those days—or my grandpa, who at the time was so broke that "the Depression didn't affect us at all." He worked for his father, James Cannon, sweeping floors and doing various odd jobs around "The Shed," their little shop located in the backyard of their family home. James ran a small business inventing various gadgets and parts that were to be used for electrical purposes.

Despite the financial shortcomings of Bob's life, in the end, Betty could not resist Bob's unmistakable charms, his ethic of hard work and honesty. So, she took a gamble on him, and they married in 1938.

The Cannon family—my maternal grandfather's forbears—emigrated from the Isle of Man in the UK to Utah in the mid 1800s, where they would join the Mormon church. Martha Hughes Cannon, James Cannon's mother, was the fourth of six wives in her polygamous marriage to Angus M. Cannon. She was a women's rights advocate, suffragist, physician and devoted Mormon. A strong-willed woman, she probably didn't appreciate playing fourth fiddle for husband Angus, and she ended up running against him for the Utah State Senate. In 1896 Martha "Mattie" Cannon made history by defeating her husband to become the first female state senator in United States history.

As it turned out, Mattie's son James, my great-grandfather, had no use for the Mormon religion, or any religion for that matter. He left Utah to settle in southern California in the early 1900s.

Though James had dropped out of school in the ninth grade, his son, my grandpa Bob, described him as a genius. In 1915, working sometimes deep into the night in his little shop in Los Angeles, James went on to invent an electrical part that would eventually be used around the world. It was called a Cannon Plug, the most common example of which can be found today on the back of a computer, where printers, for example, are connected. They're the plugs that have rows of little holes on one side, called the female, and on the other side are rows of little pins, called the male. (Great-Grandpa and Grandpa are probably rolling over in their graves with that description.) After Great-Grandpa James invented this little plug, his business began to grow.

The plugs were sold primarily to manufacturers of microphones, and eventually to airplane manufacturers back in the days leading up to World War II. Grandpa Bob, promoted from shop sweeper, would call on these customers as a representative of Cannon Electric, the official name of their fledgling manufacturing company. Cannon Electric would also produce electrical connectors for the movie studios in Hollywood, including Paramount and Fox. Over time, Cannon Electric grew substantially, and Cannon Plugs would quietly participate in many of our country's historical milestones, including in a microphone used by John F. Kennedy during his historic presidential run, and on the lunar module of the USA's famous moon landing.* [For a complete history of the company, visit the *about* page on *ittcannon.com*.] The company grew, eventually opening several manufacturing facilities in the UK, Germany, France, Australia, and Japan.

As often happens when companies become larger, the attendant problems also grew. As president of the company, James may have been a genius inventor, but he had not been formally trained in how to organize and run a company; operating the business was not one of his strong suits. He also unfortunately suffered from severe alcoholism.

Though I believe he had a kind heart, given the way my grandpa shared fond memories of him, James was prone to outbursts of anger, and according to Grandpa, was often hard to work with. By 1949, a few years after the end of the war, Cannon Electric was in the red, and nearly out of business. The main cause of this near-failure was James' ineptitude in running the business.

Though he repeatedly tried, Grandpa could not convince his dad to run things differently, to make the changes needed to improve the company. In fact, Grandpa grew so frustrated working for his dad that he finally gave up. He began to make plans with my grandma Betty to leave the company and find another line of work. This is when fate stepped in to play a big hand.

Just before the company went completely kaput, Great-Grandpa James got sick and did not recover. He made his transition (passed away) on February 20, 1950, as a result of cirrhosis of the liver. This event would thrust my grandfather Bob into the role of president of Cannon Electric at the tender age of thirty-six.

Despite completing fewer than two years of community college, it turned out Grandpa had a knack for running a business. He was able to turn Cannon Electric around and make it profitable. Over the course of the next fourteen years, the company prospered, but not without a lot of hard work and struggle on Grandpa's part.

Years later, he would openly share his self-doubts in a short memoir titled *MBAs We Weren't*, lamenting about how successful the company could have been if either he or his dad James had had a formal business education.

By 1964, Grandpa was worn out, and he ultimately decided to sell the company to ITT. Though the sale price was large by anyone's standards—in the several millions—it was no Powerball jackpot. It was sufficient for a very comfortable retirement and enough for both of them to be uncommonly generous with their children and grandchildren. He and Grandma shared their wealth while they were both still alive, rather than waiting until they passed, like most people. They gifted the maximum amount of money allowable tax free—ten thousand dollars for each grandparent, twenty thousand total—to every child and grandchild every year. I remember Grandpa telling me he thought the government was completely wasteful and inefficient, and wanted to give it as little in taxes as he possibly could. That's where the finances came from that allowed me to live down-and-out in Mill Valley years later.

As was common in those days, Grandma Betty had given up her career as a journalist in order to be supportive while Grandpa built up the business. She was a lovely, gentle woman, and I was very fond of her. Her response to many of my plans and schemes as a young boy was always a gentle, "Oh, dear."

In general, there were not a lot of overt disagreements

or arguments between Grandma and Grandpa and the family. We were the type of family to sweep all our negativity under the rug. Everyone fell into their roles. That's why I can only speculate that Grandma might have been a bit remorseful that she had not followed her career as a journalist, despite the eventual wealth and success in the family. She played her role of devoted wife and mother with dignity, elegance and uncommon humility, but I always thought there was a sense of sadness about her.

I truly admired Grandma and Grandpa for many reasons, one of which was that they were among the relatively few people who actually achieved the American Dream. Both grew up poor, but by the time they sold Cannon Electric, they had moved into a private country club in Palm Desert, California. They played golf, and at one time had a private yacht and private plane. Grandpa sat on the boards of several big companies. They both also happened to be genuinely humble, generous and kind, notwithstanding their success, and most of the employees and staff who worked for them over the years sincerely loved them.

Yet despite all of this, on one of our visits down to "The Desert" as a teenager, I remember standing in the living room of their beautiful home on the thirteenth hole of the El Dorado Country Club when a thought occurred to me. Now, I was definitely not the sharpest tool in the shed, and was generally sleepwalking my way through my young life, but it occurred to me that something was wrong. Grandma and Grandpa did not seem happy. Not really. Retired, they spent their days eating well, reading books and playing solitaire, but there was no real joy in the house.

I thought it was rather odd. Shouldn't they be beaming, proud and happy with their life accomplishments? After all, from my point of view, they had it made. *Isn't THIS what the world teaches us all to strive for?* I asked myself. But here they were, seemingly whittling away their time, and without a real sense of joy.

Grandpa often used to sit in his recliner, quietly staring off into the distance. He was gentle, kind and powerful, like a benevolent king. I was always a little intimidated by him. Yet I asked him one day, "What are you thinking about as you sit there, staring out the window?"

He said, "I think about how I could have run the company better."

What? I thought. I was very confused, since to me he represented the pinnacle of success.

I believe this was a key moment for me on my own life's journey. It planted a seed in my mind that there is something definitely wrong with the world. I had no clue what it was, but if my grandparents couldn't be truly happy or satisfied, then who could?

I'll make no bones about it. I believe getting in touch with our innate spiritual nature is the ultimate cure to that deep nagging sense of "something is missing" that many of us feel. I believe it was this sense of lack that was at the center of my grandparents' (and my) lack of happiness. Not only were we not spiritual; hell, we weren't even religious.

With regard to religion, in short, the Cannons had none. Great-Grandpa James had abandoned Mormonism, and as far as I can tell, the subject of God and religion never came up again. It simply was never discussed or mentioned in our family.

I am surprised, given this absence of anything religious or spiritual in my early life, that I had any curiosity about it at all. But apparently I did. One day, perhaps in the early 1990s, I asked Grandpa what his thoughts were about religion and God. Back then, his word was "God's Word" to me. Grandpa was the All-Knowing in my eyes, and I would take his word as Gospel.

His response was as succinct as you can get. As far as I can remember, he just grunted and waved his hand dismissively in the air. And that was the end of the conversation.

It was good enough for me. And I would not bother with the subject again for several years, not until I would eventually be forced to.

THREE

Mom Meets Dad

W ITH REGARD to politics, the Cannons leaned towards the conservative side of things. That is
why I always thought it unusual that my mom,
Janis Cannon, daughter of Bob and Betty, chose to attend
college at UC Berkeley in the 1960s. Talk about a fish out
of water. She was young and beautiful and completely in
the minority on the Cal campus—a conservative-minded
student who became part of the campus Greek system.
As one may recall, Berkeley was *the* hotbed for the liberal
free speech movement in the '60s, and I have to imagine
it was tough to be a conservative on campus then.

Though I love my mom for a lot of reasons, one of
her features I admire most is that she is utterly fearless
when it comes to saying what's on her mind, no matter
how anyone is going to take it. My favorite story is about
the day when she was sitting in a classroom as a large,
passionate discussion was raging about a current hot so-
cio-political issue. I believe there was even a guest speaker of some renown who was there to champion the cause.

Sitting in the back, Mom tentatively raised her hand

in the air and waited to be called upon. When her turn to speak finally came, she said, "I think you all just use these issues and these protests as an excuse to skip class and smoke grass!" Crickets — the whole room was stunned into silence. That's Mom.

Mom would play a large but quiet role in my healing and recovery many years down the road, so I'll share more about her a little later on. But her first order of business was making me. In order to do that, she had to meet someone, and she eventually did at Cal. His name was Jim Bundschu, a fellow conservative-minded person in the Cal Greek system.

While they may have shared a similar political outlook, and a similar religious outlook (both had none), in many ways they were quite different. Notably, while Mom came from the big city (LA) and a private school upbringing, Dad hailed from a small northern California farming town (Sonoma) and attended public school. Mom was used to Rodeo Drive and convertibles, and Dad was used to cattle drives and... well, I guess Dad had a convertible, too (a 1967 GTO). It doesn't really matter.

I don't want to get all sappy and say they "fell madly in love," because I'm not sure that is how they would describe it. I'll just say that one day they shared a laugh—both are famous for their great sense of humor—and a mutual attraction, and the next they were walking down the aisle. Dad eventually graduated, and mom left school early to stay with him. They got married in Los Angeles in 1967, settled in Sonoma, and they started a family soon after.

There's one thing I do know for sure. It took Mom time to adjust to both small-town Sonoma and to "the Far-kles," the name Dad loves to call the Bundschu family.

FOUR

The Bundschus
(Dad's side of the family)

T HE STORY of my father's side of the family, the Bundschus, and our family winery, is actually known by quite a few people—or they've at least heard it. I'm not sure how much people remember (I can barely remember what I had for dinner last night). I know this because, it is my job, as a tour guide at our family winery Gundlach Bundschu (*gun • lock-bunch • you*) Winery, to tell the story to visitors. And mysteriously, it seems people are genuinely interested in hearing our history.

As stories go, it's not a bad one. Like the Cannon story, a book could probably be written about the Bundschu side of the family, too. The story includes multiple generations, with great success and tremendous loss along the way.

It all began with my great-great-great-grandfather, Jacob Gundlach, a fourth-generation winemaker from Aschaffenburg, Germany. In the late 1840s, young Jacob asked his childhood sweetheart, Eva Hofmann, for her hand in marriage. She said yes. But her father denied Jacob permission to marry his daughter, because Jacob had no business prospects.

Now, I can't say for sure, but I believe this was a major contributor to Jacob's saying *"To hell with it"* and looking elsewhere for his future. The California Gold Rush was in full swing, and many Germans were setting sail for the New World in order to strike it rich. Jacob decided he was going to be one of them. He set sail from Germany on November 10, 1850.

After having sailed across the Atlantic and around South America, Jacob's ship arrived in San Francisco on November 10, 1851, one year to the day from his departure. Along the journey, Jacob survived a shipwreck off the coast of Africa, and was later stranded in Rio de Janeiro. He wrote in his journals that he wouldn't wish such a trip on his worst enemy.

I joke on my wine tours that people should remember this story when they fly home from their visit to wine country, and it will make the trip seem much easier.

As it turns out, Jacob arrived too late to take part in the gold rush, and he ultimately decided to make beer instead—a wise move, given all the thirsty miners and gamblers hovering around The City. His brewery, the Bavarian Brewing Company, established in 1852, did well enough that only a few years later, in the spring of 1858, Jacob was able to purchase a bit more than 400 acres of property in Sonoma, located about an hour north of San Francisco. He called his new vineyard site Rhinefarm, after the Rhine Valley in Germany. He then set up his wine-making facility in San Francisco, thus becoming only the second commercial winery in the state of California. (Buena Vista Winery in Sonoma, established six months before in 1857, was the first).

As a successful businessman, Jacob fit into early San Francisco society well, including membership in the German Benevolent Society. But in being a member of society, it often helps to have a woman beside you.

Fortunately, as it turns out, Jacob also had a romantic streak, so after purchasing Rhinefarm, and despite the risk, Jacob decided to sail all the way back to Germany, where he once again asked for permission to marry Eva Hofmann. This time, her father agreed. The two were married on July 4th, 1858.

While on their honeymoon, Eva and Jacob collected several varieties of grapevines they would need to establish Jacob's new vineyard back in California. In fact, one of the varietals they brought with them was Gewürztraminer, a varietal the family have been growing on Rhinefarm every year since. This meant that after safely returning to California with grapevines in tow, Jacob and Eva were already on their way to establishing a prosperous business.

J. Gundlach & Co. produced its first vintage of wine in 1863 and quickly began to flourish. By 1868, the business had grown large enough that Jacob needed help managing his operation. This is when he met Charles Bundschu, who was working in the produce industry. Jacob hired him to manage his business operations, a position for which he proved quite capable.

Charles was more than twenty years Jacob's junior, young enough to be Jacob's son, or, in this case, his son-in-law, which eventually became the case when he married their oldest daughter Francisca in 1875. Francisca was named after the city of San Francisco. (Her name also happens to be the answer to a quiz I give on my wine tours. The winner gets a double pour of Cabernet!)

Together, Jacob and Charles did quite well. By the turn of the century, around 1900, J. Gundlach and Co., which had now turned into Gundlach Bundschu Wine Co., now produced approximately three hundred thousand cases of wine a year. With offices in New York and New Orleans, they were shipping fine wines and brandies around the world. All this abruptly changed on the fateful day of April 18, 1906.

The great San Francisco earthquake and fire struck at 5:12 a.m. that day, with aftershocks following. Over seventy percent of The City was destroyed, including the winery production facility and three family homes. According to Charles' journals, over a million gallons of wine were lost, with a river of red wine flowing down the street and dumping into the Bay.

This was a disaster Jacob did not live to see, as he had passed a few years earlier. Though Eva, Charles, Francisca and our family survived the catastrophe, Charles, now much older, never fully recovered from watching his life's work burn to the ground. After the earthquake, the entire family relocated north, to Sonoma, where they would begin to pick up the pieces.

The third generation of the Bundschus was Walter Bundschu, son of Charles and Francisca. He and his wife Sadie Towle reopened the winery on Rhinefarm in Sonoma on a much smaller scale. They enjoyed a few years of modest success until 1919, when the Eighteenth Amendment was passed and Prohibition began.

Walter and Sadie were forced to shut down the winery and transform Rhinefarm into an actual farm, where pears were the primary crop, with tomatoes and hay grown as well. They also were able to continue growing wine grapes, but these were sold to other wineries that were producing wine for the Catholic Church. I always offer a toast to the Catholics on my tours for helping our family stay afloat during the lean years.

Walter passed away prematurely in 1938, in his forties. This is when my grandfather, Walter and Sadie's son Towle, at the tender age of nineteen, left college early to come home and help run the farm. A couple of years later, Grandpa met Mary Crumrine, a graduate of Pomona College, and a farmer's daughter. They were married in 1942, the same year Grandpa was drafted into the Army, where he served in WWII as an aerial gunner. He came home from the war a couple of years later and took on his responsibilities at Rhinefarm.

Grandpa Towle was well-loved by many around him. A rugged farmer and outdoors man, he spent his years working long hours tending to the crops on Rhinefarm and raising a family with Grandma Mary. They had three children, my dad Jim being the oldest, then Susan, and Gigi. Though I don't remember too much about Grandpa Towle (unfortunately he passed when I was a very young boy), he is said to have had a great sense of humor and was known to throw some wonderful parties.

My mom shares fond memories of him and says he was one of her favorites. I call him the unsung hero in our family because of all the hard work he did to maintain Rhinefarm. There was no winery on the property until the last couple of years of his life, and so his part of our company history can often be overlooked. But without him and his years of hard work, Gundlach Bundschu wouldn't be around today.

Grandma Mary would live many years after Grandpa Towle. By then, she was the matriarch of our family, and would hold court in her kitchen on Rhinefarm every day. Early every morning, she and Dad would meet to share a cup of coffee and discuss life and the family, and what needed to be done around the property. She was always there with a warm smile and a kind word. Today, her house, which is the office and event center of the business, is affectionately known by employees and visitors alike as "Mary's House" in her honor.

In my mid-twenties, I was working as the national sales manager for the winery. Grandma noticed that, due to my shyness, I rarely spoke up in meetings. She made a point of repeatedly encouraging me to speak up more, and to share my voice. Though this was my personal experience, I know she also shared a lot of love with my brother, sister and cousins as well.

This is not to say that Grandma was always lovey-dovey. She was full of fire, and could be quite opinionated as well. She often engaged in elaborate debates with my brother Jeff about this or that.

Grandma also seemed to be quite aware that I had drinking issues in my early twenties, when partying was still my favorite thing to do. Though I didn't recognize it at the time, I look back and realize that she was worried about me. She often commented on the dark circles under my eyes on Monday mornings, and suggested I take better care of myself. I just brushed it off. She once gave me a poster that read, "Those who hoot with the owls at night cannot fly with the eagles at dawn." Needless to say, I didn't hang that one up.

Grandma did have one characteristic that she did not share with anyone else in the family. She was a practicing Christian, an Episcopalian. And that is about all I know regarding her involvement. As I said earlier, religion was not a big thing in our family, which may have been why Grandma kept her spiritual beliefs to herself. Whatever did come up about "God" was water off a duck's back; I wanted nothing to do with it, and neither did my dad or anyone else, as far as I can remember.

My religion was drinking and having a good time, and denying and repressing an extraordinary amount of guilt and fear that would ultimately surface and bury me. Grandma knew all this about me and everyone else in our family, so she never talked about religion. All of this is a way of saying that Grandma was a very loving and strong presence in my life, and the lives of my family. She is missed by all of us around Rhinefarm who remember her.

During Towle and Mary's time together, they would farm Rhinefarm for over thirty years. In the late sixties, after finishing college, Dad approached Grandpa Towle and asked if he could restart the winery and resurrect the old Gundlach Bundschu family brand name. Grandpa thought about it, and he said no! It appears he was doubtful that a young "whipper snapper" like Dad, who was in his early twenties, could carry off relaunching a winery associated with our old family heritage.

Nevertheless, Dad was persistent, and he would eventually produce a batch of wine with John Merritt and Barney Fernandez in the kitchen of our little bungalow, located a couple hundred feet from Mary's House on Rhinefarm. John and Barney would later become my uncles, with John marrying my Aunt Susan, and Barney taking Aunt Gigi as his bride.

As the story goes, the young wine-making team invited Grandpa and Grandma over to the bungalow to try out their new wine on Halloween night in 1969. Let's say they ended up drinking more than one bottle, and Grandpa was impressed enough that he changed his mind. Yes, Dad could use the old family name.

A few years later, after plowing under the pear orchard and replanting Rhinefarm with wine grapes, Gundlach Bundschu Winery opened its doors in 1976 for the first time in over fifty years.

Dad ran the winery with a strong *work hard / play hard* ethic. A farmer at heart, I remember him being up early every morning and heading to work out into the vineyard. And when I say early, I mean *early*, sometimes meeting with local farmers down at "The Lazy D" at 4:30 a.m. to have breakfast before going off to work. I know firsthand that this is true, because I remember him dragging Jeff and me out of bed to go with him once or twice. The hard work, including hiring great winemakers and a terrific team of people, would pay off, though, and open the door to a successful business.

Over the ensuing years, "Gun Bun" grew and became known for its bold Cabs and Zins and classic Gewürztraminer, as well as its penchant for creative and outlandish promotional escapades. For instance, Dad and a group of local Sonoma "Wine Patrollers" once raided the Napa Valley Wine Train in capes and masks and poured all the guests on board Sonoma Valley wines. Another, somewhat bolder move, happened when our then-winemaker Lance Cutler learned that Sir Richard Branson (of Virgin Airlines) was visiting California wine country, and he planned to spend his entire day in Napa, which is traditionally the better known wine region. Well, Lance Cutler, appalled at the news, organized a hijacking of Mr. Branson's bus, and directed it over the hill into Sonoma and to our winery, so Mr. Branson could try our Sonoma wines. Such bold and adventurous moves would lead to recognition for Dad and Lance, along with several other fellow

Sonoma vintners. They were eventually acknowledged for helping to promote Sonoma Valley and Sonoma County wines.

I think it's pretty clear the spirit of Bacchus was alive and well at our winery in its early years. The "play hard" aspect of our family and business involved a lot of parties and celebrations. Many long-time wine club members could share a story or two about our penchant for fun and revelry. You can be sure a lot of wine, and occasionally a little tequila, were part of the festivities.

Bacchus is the Roman god of wine. Known as the god of ritual madness and ecstasy, ancient Romans used to practice wild hedonistic rituals referred to as Bacchanalia. Now, Gun Bun was not this extreme, but I would say there was a touch of Bacchus in our company spirit. Indeed, in Gun Bun's early history, we branded ourselves Bacchus Wines, and today one can join the Bacchus Club—our wine club.

I bring this up because it seems I am the only one in the Bundschu family who took our old Bacchanalian religion to heart. I drank hard and often—more than anyone else in the family, and while I never attended any orgiastic parties (part of the old Bacchanalian rituals), I did hope, after having a few, to hook up with a young woman now and again. As I said, getting lit and having fun (and denying an ocean of guilt) was *the way* for me.

Today, things have changed quite a bit at Gundlach Bundschu. Under my brother Jeff's leadership—he serves as the company president—I would say that we have shifted our company focus. While at one time the two main concerns were making good wine and having a good time, our first priority now is making great wine, and the second is making people happy. We still have a good time, but now our focus is on producing outstanding wine, and then providing great experiences that complement the wine.

Though we consider ourselves to be primarily a Bordeaux producer, meaning our focus is on Cabernet Sauvignon and Merlot, we produce over ten different varietals of wine. And thanks to the stellar vineyard crew, led by my cousin Towle Merritt and Abel Amezquita, and our exceptional winemaking team, led by Keith Emerson, Joe Uhr, and Luies Gallegos, I'm happy to report that most visitors tell me they love all our wines. In short, it takes much hard work, blood, sweat and tears to both produce great wine and then sell and market it to the world.

I would just like to summarize by giving thanks to everyone who chooses to work at Gun Bun, because that choice includes being part of the Bundschu family. It's the people, and the truly collaborative effort on everyone's part, and everyone's heart, that make it possible to produce and market great wines.

I can't mention "making people happy" without sharing about Gun Bun's love of music. It started with Dad sitting at home, practicing his saxophone for hours on end, and then progressed with Jeff, who played bass guitar in a band in college. Jeff would eventually be inspired to bring his (and our) love of music to the winery.

For over ten years, we have hosted a music festival called Huichica Music Festival, where we invite fifteen to twenty bands, along with all different kinds of food trucks, and sellers of beer and cider. These warm, breezy afternoons are filled with people milling around, grooving to music, with tumblers of wine in hand and hopefully not a care in the world. Mostly indie acts and folk rock, the music attracts music aficionados from all over the country. While HMF happens in June, we host small, intimate concerts all year round, where people can get up close and personal with their favorite indie band, glass of wine in hand.

As I've mentioned, growing up in our home, there was not a lot of time spent thinking about or talking about religion. We followed the more secular philosophy of working hard and doing the right thing by people.

There was, though, one doctrine that was passed around by Grandma that must be mentioned: Hear No Evil, Speak No Evil, See No Evil. Yes it was those statuettes of three little monkeys that were popular in the '60s and '70s; one monkey covering its ears, one covering its mouth, and the other covering its eyes. Dad said Grandma first gave him the monkeys to take to college with him. Later, she gave one to all my cousins, my brother and sister, and me. No doubt Grandma's intent with this message was good. I believe the message was that we should seek to overlook the "sins" of others, and in ourselves, and instead put our focus on the good in people.

Looking back, it's clear that growing up I took the message of the monkeys in a much different way. I took it to mean I should deny all my negative feelings and emotions—stuff them way down deep, and pretend that they were not there. I believed I was always supposed to be "happy-go-lucky." Hence, I grew up taking my perception of the monkey philosophy to heart, and it would end up being both my worst mistake and the greatest thing that ever happened to me.

FIVE

My First Memory

M Y FIRST memory is going to the beach with my mom and my grandmother, Betty Cannon, sometime in the early '70s. My brother Jeff and my cousins Chris and Kasey were probably there, too. My father and Grandpa were, in all likelihood, off having Grandpa's favorite highballs at the Santa Monica Beach Club, where my grandparents were members. I was playing in the sand with a little plastic bucket and shovel.

What I remember about that day is the distinct feeling of aloneness I felt while I played. I was in my own little world, and did not really feel connected to my mom or anyone else around me. I didn't even notice them. I share this brief memory (in this brief chapter) because this subtle sense of isolation and aloneness would follow me well into adulthood, coloring my experience of the world. Though I would eventually make friends, play sports, etc. and have a normal social life externally, internally I would always feel deeply alone and separate.

The good news, at least for my mom, was that I was easy to babysit. Give me a bucket and a shovel or a few toys, and I could entertain myself for hours.

SIX

The Force is Strong with This One

Yet within you is a Force that no illusions can resist.
— A Course in Miracles T-22.V.5.4

O VER THE YEARS, many people have asked me what it was like to grow up on a vineyard. Though I actually haven't said so, I want to say, "It was like growing up anywhere else, except we had a bigger backyard."

We were a regular family. Usually we got along, but sometimes there were struggles. Sometimes major struggles. We definitely had our share of dysfunction. But what family doesn't have dysfunction?

We had to go to school every day and do homework (in theory). We had dogs and cats, and we kids had to do chores around the house. After school, we would ride our bikes around the ranch or go shoot birds with a BB gun. I know that sounds bad, but it was the '70s. We were typical, mischievous young boys, just like in eras past. Occasionally we liked to take a break from it all and go to the movies.

I was six years old in 1977, when my parents took

me to see the opening of a new space adventure movie with the strange name *Star Wars* (I wondered—*Do stars go to war?*). We entered a packed house in our small town movie house, the Sebastiani Theater. The Sebastiani is an old style theater with one big screen, high ceilings, elaborate wall decorations and beautifully upholstered wooden chairs. We got seats up in the balcony and I sat down with little to no expectations.

The lights dimmed, the sound hushed. Then: "Daaa, Daaa, DaDaDa Daa Daa ..." That glorious symphonic beginning to the famous movie boomed through the theater. Moments later, after that scroll of words describing the plot (which I couldn't read), the well-known opening scene—with the small rebel ship being chased and attacked by the huge, omnipresent, never-ending Imperial Star Destroyer—unfolded across the screen with all its magic and glory, and I was hooked forever.

To this day, I have never left a theater more mesmerized and excited as I was leaving that first screening of *Star Wars*. Like so many millions of others, my love of *Star Wars* is deep and has stayed with me even into middle age.

The reason I bring up *Star Wars* is that I believe that it was the first mystical experience of my life. On a superficial level, I loved the movie for all the spaceships and laser fights. I loved the two 'droids—R2D2 and C3PO—and their journey on the adventure. And on some level, I identified with Luke Skywalker, the farm boy who dreamed of flying fighters for the Rebel Fleet. Though my own future involved working on a grape farm, I, too, would dream of one day becoming a pilot. But I'm certain now that I also loved the movie for a deeper and more subtle reason. (It's also my theory as to why the *Star Wars* movie franchise is still so popular today, over forty years later).

I was by nature a very introverted, shy kid, and in truth, I did not think much of myself. Sadness seemed to be built into my personality. Yes, a therapist could (and eventually would) point out that there were external circumstances that contributed to my depressive state of mind, but in the end, I peg it to my own internal personality. And eventually, studying and applying what I learned in *A Course in Miracles* would help me put the "blame" for my sadness where it truly belongs—in my own mind.

But I have to say, being a powerless little boy in a big powerful world, with no belief in, or awareness of, any sort of higher power, I know that *The Force*—a concept central to the *Star Wars* mythology—affected me in a deep and profound way. In short, it was what I believe to be my very first introduction to the idea of a Higher Power—or a power that exists beyond normal human confines.

"It [The Force] is an energy field created by all living things. It surrounds us and penetrates us; it binds the galaxy together." —Obi-Wan Kenobi, *Star Wars: A New Hope*

Who wouldn't want to harness the power of The Force, like the Jedi Knights in the movie? Though, as I said, I consciously loved the movie for the "war" part of *Star Wars*—spaceships, people blasting each other to smithereens, all the characters and the hero's journey plot—I am certain that on a deeper, unconscious level of my mind, the presence of The Force in the movie, and in all the *Star Wars* movies, is what made these films such a powerful force in my own life (pun intended). The idea of a Higher Power like The Force planted the seed that such a thing even existed—and perhaps opened the first little crack in my otherwise completely closed mind.

—Before I return to the main narrative of my life, there are some things I feel I need to share. This next section, while it might seem to be a departure from the whole fabric of the story, is really an essential bridge to what occurred later on. I feel it's necessary to explain these internal thoughts —unseen except by me—because they greatly contributed to the whole of my life. —

In speaking of a power or a force that had a pretty big presence in my young life, I feel I should share something about another power that had captured my young mind —a darker power.

Though I was not raised Christian, or religious, I couldn't help but hear much of the Christian theology growing up, including the great power of the Devil, or Satan. I had little interest in learning about God, and *no* interest in learning about Jesus, but I was rather fascinated by the concept of the Devil. I would say that in my young life I obsessed, if quietly, about the Devil. I'd heard what many Christians teach—that if you're not a Christian, you are doomed to go to hell after you die, to spend the rest of eternity with Satan, who will torture you forever and forever.

Well, I thought, *I'm not a Christian. And I'm not a good boy. And I have no idea who's right about the afterlife, Christians or atheists or whoever. What if the Christians are right?*

I took this train of thought very seriously. In fact, my belief in this idea of eternal damnation began to grow in me as time went by. Along the way, several incidents occurred in my life which seemed to validate this frightening belief in the Devil.

I remember one incident on an afternoon when we were around nine or ten years old. My mischievous friend and neighbor Ricardo—who I think was Catholic, but I can't be sure—decided to have a little fun with me, and he told me a story about the Devil. I don't remember the details of the story—it may have been about a seance where the Devil showed up, or something like that—but the point of the story was that the Devil is real and active. Being the gullible person that I am, as I was listening to this story, I remember Ricardo getting more and more animated as he went along. He could see he "had me." He must have seen the fear in my eyes as he spoke, because he was clearly having a ball. And no doubt about it—I was rattled.

And that wasn't the only story. Another friend of mine told a similar story a few years later, and again I was quietly terrified inside. *What if all this is true!?* The point is, I would end up having a real fear of hell and Satan growing up. I'm not sure, but I think this may be a common fear in the world.

I bring up these stories because apparently my fear and belief in the Devil ran pretty deep, and I believe it contributed to what I would experience just a few years down the road. It wound up being a case of "the thing which I greatly feared is come upon me." In other words, "What you are afraid of will happen."

Another key moment on my journey happened in my adolescence, when I was sitting in class at school one day. As I often did, I drifted off from the lesson and instead looked around at the students. They all looked so calm and certain, compared to the way I felt about myself inside. The little voice in my mind that was always judging and comparing, equated me as "inferior" to all the kids in the class. And I believed it. I really thought I was "below" everyone. And I seemed to have perfected my ability to dismiss anyone who ever tried to tell me I was good or special in any way. The little voice would have none of it. I was *the worst*.

And so sitting there that day, my great wish, or dream, was to just be an equal to my peers, to *feel* equal to all my peers. I never wanted to be "better" than anyone, because that might cause envy, and I *couldn't stand* envy. I just wanted to perceive myself as equal.

I would learn many years later in *A Course in Miracles* that in this world, it is literally impossible to perceive equality. Everyone seems to be inferior or superior to another in some way. At least, if we're honest with ourselves, that's how the mind judges. I think superficially people believe there is equality in the world, but anyone willing to look under the hood of their own psyche will learn that there is some serious judgement going on. God knows that in a few years I would do just this—look under my own hood. And I was aghast to learn what I found out.

In short, I would one day be absolutely horrified to learn that deep in my own unconscious mind, I believed I was not inferior to others, but *superior* to everyone! After all those years of inner "woe-is-me, look how little and small I am compared to others," I would learn that I secretly—even to myself—thought that I was better than everyone! Wow!

The reasoning behind this thinking had something to do with my faith in my own littleness. "Look how meek I am." (Read "special.") "I'm the meekest person in the whole world! And didn't Jesus say the meek shall inherit the earth?"

See where this is going? I was aghast to learn that in the end, I did think I was superior to everyone. Never mind that to the outside world, I was clearly somewhere in the middle. An okay student, but nowhere near the top. A good athlete, but no high school MVP awards for me. A few brain cells upstairs, but certainly no Mensa people came knocking at my door.

Thankfully, this wholly false belief or fantasy wouldn't hold up for long. What I would learn on my spiritual journey would put an end to it. But before all these insights, for many years I would occasionally, quietly and almost unconsciously, wish for equality. I bring this up because it is my understanding that this *wish* may have contributed to my actually finding a way to perceive myself as equal to everyone—without thinking I was crazy. Or maybe better, my wish opened the door to my being led or guided to a way in which I could perceive the perfect equality of all people.

How am *I* equal to Mother Teresa? Impossible, you say? Well, I obviously didn't think I was, either. But nevertheless, a way to perceive myself as perfectly equal to her and everyone else *did* come to me, and I'll share more about that later.

Now that I've given this background, I'll continue on with the narrative of the story.

SEVEN

Are You There God?
It's Me, Robbie

I AM WALKING briskly across campus on a chilly fall morning. A pack of students pass by me, laughing and shoving each other around. Off in the distance, others stand in line to get a snack at the snack window. Meanwhile, I keep moving. I don't want anyone to notice that I am alone.

I am in eighth grade, and I have no friends. Literally, no friends. At least at school.

It wasn't always this way. Through most of my young life, I had friends to play with. Sometimes a friendship would end, and a new one would develop, but I always had someone. Making friends seemed to come easily enough. I was never a loner. I was never popular, either. I was just an average little kid. At least that is how I felt.

But that all changed after I arrived in middle school. In sixth grade, my best friend had rejected me one day at school on a cool foggy morning. Just like that. He had found a new friend and had started hanging out with him. The writing was probably on the wall, but my power to deny reality was out of this world. And so on that cold morning, as I approached the two of them standing near a tetherball court, they both looked at me and said, "Get lost. We don't want you around anymore." Old school. No ghosting here. Right between the eyes. I was shocked, and to say it was a gut punch is the understatement of the century.

I managed to hide my complete and total devastation in that moment and for the rest of that day at school. But when I got home, I locked myself in our guest bathroom so no one would hear me, and simply broke down. I cried, or rather bawled, to the deepest depths of my soul.

When the flow of tears finally began to ebb, a deep resolve began to grow in me, until it became a full force. I stood up straight, clenched my fists, peered at myself in the mirror *hard* straight into my own eyes, and declared with complete and absolute conviction, "No one gets in."

Then I unlocked the door, walked out of the bathroom, and acted as if nothing had ever happened.

No doubt, this event affected all my relationships going forward in some deep, profound, mysterious way. Let's just say I lost my ability to trust that day, and so I was less willing to make friends. At least in the immediate future.

And so for the next two years in middle school, excluding a brief, rootless friendship in seventh grade, I was a bonafide loner. Every day during break and lunchtime, I would walk around the big public school campus alone, around the far corners, back across the middle, always moving. Didn't want anyone to notice that I was alone. They probably did.

I have no recollection what was going on at home. I don't think anyone in my family was the wiser. My situation at school for those two years was my little secret.

I was clearly troubled at this time. I got sent home one day after getting into a fight. A popular kid who was part of a rat pack used to always steal donuts right out of my hand as I walked across campus. He'd literally rip whatever part of the donut that wasn't physically in my fist and shove it straight into his mouth. One winter day, during a break, he kicked me across the chest while he was playing around with a friend. I looked down and saw a big swath of fresh mud stuck all over the front of my brand-new parka.

I *exploded*. I took off my jacket and handed it to a kid nearby. Then, screaming expletives at him at the top of my lungs, I started shoving him backwards, *hard*, in a rage. He looked completely shocked and terrified, as this attack seemed to come out of nowhere.

A curious thing then happened. During my fit of rage, as I was forcefully shoving him, *knowing* I could really do some serious damage (all those years of wrestling with my bigger, older brother gave me loads of confidence), it suddenly dawned on me that I could not do it. I couldn't punch him in the face or hurt him in any way. Something within me stopped me.

Meanwhile, I was in a pickle. I knew I wasn't going to hurt him, but now all the kids were standing around, watching the spectacle. What was I going to do now? Then out of nowhere, a teacher showed up and saved the day! He broke up the fight and sent us both to the principal's office.

I was sent home that day, and I remember during our family dinner that night Dad seemed really happy and excited to hear I'd been in a fight. He wanted all the details. (We Bundschus are *not* known as the biggest fighters).

Another time, I was apparently a bad troublemaker in my eighth-grade English class. I continually harassed the teacher and caused all kinds of trouble until they had to call in my mother. Needless to say, I wasn't doing well at this time.

And yet, in the middle of all this middle school drama, one day I made a huge discovery. Slinking around campus alone during lunch break as usual, I suddenly got the idea to go check out the campus library. So I walk into the relatively large building situated right in the center of campus, and lo and behold, I discovered that there were absolutely no students in there. None. I had the place to myself! This was a major discovery. Needless to say, this is where I began to come and hide every day during lunch period.

Looking ahead, one might think this is the point in the story where my love of reading and books would begin. But my true love of books actually began with my stepmom Nancy, who was a schoolteacher. A year or two before, she had given me the classic book *The Lion, The*

Witch, and the Wardrobe by C.S. Lewis, and she used to read it to me every night before bed. I loved that story and reading it with Nancy. I was blessed with a vivid imagination, so I learned I could really get into stories like this one. Thus reading with Nancy is where my love of books and reading actually began. I am so grateful to her for this.

One interesting side note. I didn't have a clue *The Lion, The Witch, and the Wardrobe* was a Christian-themed book, a story about sacrifice. It seems Christianity, in one form or another, was always following me around, whether I wanted it to or not.

Back to the library. I learned on that first day that there was only one other person in there, the librarian. He was a quiet, older man, and we didn't talk at all when I entered the large room, at least not that I can remember. It was filled with rows and rows of shelves full of books, a couple of long tables with little plastic chairs for the kids, and the desk where he stood.

I immediately went to the stacks and started browsing the books. I would find one that sounded interesting, and pluck it off the shelf and start reading, until the lunch bell rang, signaling the end of lunch. I don't remember the first few books I encountered, or any books I would read in that library for that matter, except one.

One day I plucked a title off the shelf by an author named Judy Blume. The title of the book was *Are You There God? It's Me, Margaret.* Then I sat down and began to read. It didn't take long to figure out that it was a story about a girl. I didn't care. I don't think I knew it was a story written for girls, and if I did, I didn't care about that, either. I had always liked girls. For some reason I felt more comfortable around them than little boys. I could be myself around them more. I had made many casual friendships with girls in my classes over my years in school. Thus a story about a girl and her problems didn't faze me at all.

I read the book in there all the way through. The book was all about her relationship with God, and her relationship struggles with classmates and growing up. I had no relationship with God at this time, and wanted nothing to do with this "God" business. Nevertheless, it is remarkable to me that I still read and enjoyed the story so much. Her character had problems with kids at school. I had problems with kids at school. And so I really enjoyed this book.

Today I would say that finding and reading a book with God as a central character in the book was all part of a greater plan that I could not have seen at the time. As I will share more about a little later on, I believe we are all on a journey of awakening. And what I'll call for now our True Self is guiding us all along the way. I know that may sound crazy to some. But please hang with me. All I can say is that there is *so* much going on in our lives most of us are not even aware of. In the case of Margaret and God, a little seed was being planted about a Higher Power. I had no clue at the time, of course.

Though this was a little chapter in my life story, I believe it was pretty powerful. After all, the overall arc of my journey has been to find a spiritual path. Finding and reading a book featuring God at such a young age when I had *no* interest in God at the time (at least consciously) is a pretty cool thing.

EIGHT

Working on Rhinefarm

WHILE IT'S TRUE that I was lucky to be raised on a vineyard, it didn't always feel that way. Dad is a farmer at heart. He would take us out into the vineyard often, even when we were quite young. And I believe he hoped his children would share his love of farming, which is why he had us doing full-time work out in the vineyards during the summers. I don't remember exactly how old I was when I started working summers in the vineyard, but I must have been around twelve or thirteen.

It's funny, but a lot of people seem to romanticize the wine business and believe those who grow up in it lead a life of privilege—similar to the wealthy old-monied people on the East Coast. I think Dad knew people might perceive us this way, which is why he worked Jeff and me, and eventually Katie, that much harder.

"So where did *you* summer this year?"

I'll tell you where I summered—out in the dirt on Rhinefarm, with a shovel in my hand!

On a typical work day, we'd wake up early in the

morning, get in Dad's pickup truck and start driving. Dad liked to puff on cigars, so the inside of his truck used to smell of dust and stale cigar smoke. Eventually my lovely, wise, and ever-thoughtful stepmom (or second Mom) Nancy, Dad's second wife, "suggested" Dad quit the cigars. I'm glad he did, even though the smoke never really bothered me.

Anyway, we'd get in his truck early and start driving. Didn't talk too much. I never knew where we were going until we got there. We were always driving to some far corner of the vineyard where there was work to be done. So we'd get to where we were going, stop, get out. Then Dad would explain what job I needed to do.

The work ranged widely. Sometimes it was a fun job, like cultivating a vineyard (driving a tractor and plowing), or driving the company garbage truck to the dump. Other times, it was a little tougher, like using a chainsaw to remove big Manzanita bushes off an old fire road in ninety-eight-degree heat, or picking up boulders to clear a field for a new vineyard.

Of course, I also spent a lot of time working with the grapevines themselves: picking grapes during harvest, pruning in the winter, and tying vines to the trellis in the spring. There was never a moment when there wasn't something to be done. The hours were long, and I have to admit that sometimes I secretly envied the kids in town who screwed around in the summer, doing things like going swimming (at least, that is what I imagined they were doing).

Because dad is a farmer and outdoorsman who loves to hunt and fish, at a very young age I believed that is what he wanted me to be. And maybe there was a bit of truth in that. It would be natural for a father to wish that his sons share his values and interests. The thing is, I assumed things that were not necessarily so. But because it was all internalized, I never thought about, nor did I know how to question or discuss with my father what he thought of his work or his passions. It never occurred to me to *ask* him what he wanted for my future. It might have helped if I'd asked him, "What is it about the work that makes you so happy?" Or "Do you want me to work for the winery for the rest of my life?"

For better or worse, though, neither Jeff, Katie, nor I turned out to be the farmer and outdoors person Dad may have wished we were. But though I tried hard, I just didn't get the inner payoff that others seemed to get after a good ol' fashioned hard day's work. I got paid, but I had no sense of pride or joy in my work, even on days when I did a really good job. And so my years of work in the vineyard were hardly romantic. I was more like a robot, coolly doing what needed to be done next. "Gotta do what Dad says."

Like so many other sons, I craved Dad's approval. And while everyone is a people-pleaser to some degree — it's how we all get by in this world — I took it to the next level. While Dad has that almost-mystical connection to the land and the vineyard, as many farmers often do, I did not have this connection, and I did not understand it. Yet I worked out in the vineyard for Dad for years as if I did. But as a young man, I didn't know what *I* loved or what *I* valued. My inner operating software said, "Do what Dad says and does. Period."

So though I tried to internalize Dad's assumed expectations, I just couldn't live up to them. (*Why don't I love this work the way Dad does?*) This feeling of being flawed in some way was a very subtle form of thinking of myself as a sinner. And because all my thinking about this was internalized and never expressed, I took it upon myself to be self-punishing. At the same time, I was, ironically, trying to escape the pain of being an unknown to myself. How could I know who I was, if I didn't even know what I wanted to be, or what I loved to do?

Bear in mind, I kept this all on the down-low. Outwardly, I almost never complained about work, and I would do the job quietly and dutifully. But inwardly, it was a different story. I was apathetic and numb, and took no joy in my work. There is no one to blame for this; it was built into my personality. And I think my reactions and inner experiences of my years working out in the vineyard speak, to some degree, of my perceived personality flaws that would eventually lead to a massive fall.

NINE

"I Have Found The Light" — My First Drunk

SPEAKING of massive falls, I think it's time to share the story about my second mystical experience. I look at it as a mystical experience now, but maybe I'd have described it a little differently a few years ago.

Though there was lots of work to be done in the vineyard, there was also lots of time to goof off. For many years, every day after school I used to play with Ricardo, the joker I mentioned earlier, and Harvey, his younger brother. They were the sons of Marcelo and Victoria Hernandez, our vineyard manager and his wife. They lived just down the lane from us on the far corner of Rhinefarm, the part of the vineyard we call La Paz.

So all of us kids used to take the bus to and from school together, and after school we would usually play all sorts of games and do things around the ranch before we were called in to dinner. We'd ride bikes or play baseball with a Wiffle bat and tennis ball. Sometimes we'd go into the old barn next to their house and test our mettle by taking turns walking tightrope style on a two-by-four beam that stretched twenty feet across the barn, fifteen feet above the floor. Thankfully, none of us ever fell off the beam onto the old dusty wooden bins that sat below.

Overall, we had a great time, and I have many fond memories of those days.

Ricardo, who was in my grade at school, was fearless, and loved getting into trouble. Being the natural follower that I was, I would usually join him in his mischievous ventures.

So one day, Ricardo and I came home from school. We must have been around twelve or thirteen years old, and it was a Monday. Ricardo's parents had just had a big party over the weekend. After we got off the bus, we were kicking around Ricardo's house when we happened upon an ice chest full of ice-cold Budweiser beer. So we—and by we I mean Ricardo—got the idea to each steal one can and go drink it somewhere. Naturally, I thought it was a fantastic idea.

We took our ice-cold beer and ran nearly a quarter of a mile through the vineyard, up on the side of the hill, above a block of Cab grapes. We found a nice shaded spot in the grass under a big bush, far away from any meddling parents. We were safe. We each cracked open our beer and took our first sip. It tasted good. Really good. I felt excited and free. We chatted and sipped and laughed without a care in the world.

When we were done, we decided, "Let's go get another one!"

And so we ran all the way back to the ice chest, each

took another beer, and returned back to the scene of the crime, where we continued to drink. We ended up repeating this process two more times, and by the end of our fourth beer, Ricardo and I were loaded. We ended up wrestling each other in the tall grass and kept rolling down the little hill over and over again, right into the big bush below us, laughing hysterically.

I had never had so much fun in my life. I simply cannot overstate how good I felt that afternoon. I didn't know it was possible to feel that good. This was my first drunk, and by far the best drunk I've ever had.

I like to call that day my second mystical experience, because it was from that time forward that I would unconsciously begin my journey of seeking happiness. As I shared earlier, I quietly suffered from depression and low self-esteem. The light, joyful experience of that first intoxication was truly an "I have found the light" moment. I would spend the next fifteen years seeking that light over and over again. Though after that afternoon, I would not drink in earnest until a few years later, I truly believed I had found the solution.

When I was young, getting drunk became the path to enlightenment for me, for sure. Between the ages of fifteen and thirty, who knows how many times I raised a glass or ten with friends on the weekends or over a holiday. In short, getting lit was the solution to that deep sense of guilt and littleness (i.e., "I am nothing") that I kept returning to over and over, and that seemed to constantly nag at me. To be sure, there were many fun nights with friends and alcohol, but they almost always came with a hangover and a load of guilt the next morning. I never quite knew what caused the guilt, but it was always there, like a cold wet blanket draped over me.

It's tempting to share a long drunk-a-log full of stories of drama, romance, utter embarrassment, and sheer luck and survival. But I won't, since this is not what this book is about. But—oh, what the hell! I'll share one or two, since drinking was such a big part of my young adult life, and it will round out the picture of this portion of it. It also shows how off-base I eventually discovered I was about being "enlightened" through alcohol.

Before we were of age, we often tried to get beer by asking older strangers in front of the Quick Stop Mini Mart if they would buy a case for us. "Excuse me, can you do me a favor?" was the classic line. Yet, often this didn't work. Our fallback plan was to drive up to Rhinefarm and sneak into the old redwood barn (currently a concert venue) on the property, where we stored unlabeled "party supply" wine that we had bottled up at the winery. It was quite a mix. There could be anything from unlabeled Pinot Noir to Johannesburg Riesling. We'd grab a couple of bottles and drive up a hill to the top of Seventh Street, a popular place for teens to hang, drink, and avoid the cops. These were simple, innocent times. But as the years passed, the drinking slowly began to progress.

I think I should point out that getting drunk was actually only half the path to enlightenment for me. What I mean is, I had only one other ambition in life besides getting lit: to find "the one." This was the other half of the enlightenment equation. It was a classic if/then situation: *if* I get drunk, *then* I will have the courage to meet a girl/talk to a girl/hook up with a girl. I mean, even a blind squirrel finds an acorn on occasion. And *then*, God willing (or God forbid), I'd meet the girl of my dreams.

When I was in high school, after watching my parents and many of their friends divorce, I told myself that I would *never* let that happen to me, and therefore, I'd *never* date a girl unless I *knew* she was "the one." I was determined not to make the same mistake as my parents. Naturally, such a restricted, and in my current opinion, unhealthy attitude resulted in me passing up opportunities to date several beautiful young women in high school, college, and beyond. Since I didn't know if they were "the one," fear won out, and I didn't make the effort to date them. Now, I'm not certain they would have even wanted to date me, but I never gave it a chance. The result of this attitude was that I went for many years without ever having a girlfriend, even though there literally was nothing I wanted more in the world.

Yet, because of my still-unknown-to-me, eff'ed-up psychological issues, when opportunity to meet a girl *did* come along, I always ran away. Looking back, I believe it was a symbol of my fear of love. (Years later, as *A Course in Miracles* student, I would learn this is actually a universal fear).

Anyway, I could share many tales of drunk-gone-wrong revelry. There was the time I hooked up with a young woman one night in San Francisco, ran into her again at my favorite bar, whispered something into her ear while she was shooting pool (I don't remember what, because I was deeply inebriated), and then literally got slapped across the face, right in front of everybody.

There was the time my college friends and I sat around a table, playing drinking games one night in Davis, until they all took off with their girlfriends. Feeling a little lonely and envious, I drove to a bar in downtown Davis by myself in order to meet a girl, and when that failed miserably, what I got instead was a DUI when I drunkenly tried to drive back home.

Then there was *that* night out in San Francisco with the fellas. (Sorry, but what happened in SF stays in SF!)

There are many other stories, some involving even greater debauchery, which I won't share because a) They're not really relevant to the spiritual journey theme of this book, and b) Because I have nieces.

But there is one more story to summarize them all. It was another Friday night in the City. As usual, I took Muni—the local bus service—over to my friend Rob's apartment (another college friend I made when I transferred from UC Davis to the University of San Francisco) because parking was a pain in the City, and I did not want another DUI. When I got there, we secured our usual twelve-pack of beer, split it between us, and while we drank, we got ready to go out. We loved to listen to music, smoke cigarettes, and get a good heat on. It was around ten p.m., still early by City standards, when it was time to go. We split a cab down to our favorite watering hole, The Blue Light on Union Street, in the heart of Cow Hollow, a popular San Francisco shopping and cafe district. We loved the Blue Light because it had a pool table in the back, and also because it was a happening place to be. We rolled into the place, found two seats at the bar, sat down, and drank.

I called it the Rob & Rob Factor. My friend Rob was tall, slender, and had a cool way about him that made him a virtual magnet for women. With him as the main attraction, we would just sit there and drink cocktails and laugh about stuff, sometimes for over an hour. And while we were doing this, the bar would slowly fill up all around us, and we just ignored everyone in the room and kept to ourselves.

Though it was not consciously planned, I believe we ended up doing the exact opposite of what many guys do at bars like these. They stand around in the corner, scope out all the women from of the corner of their eye, until they get up the nerve to talk to one or two of them. Instead, we just sat there and ignored everyone. And drank. Did I mention we drank?

By the time midnight rolled around, we'd end up out of our chairs, shooting pool, or maybe talking to a couple of the women who were there. God only knows, because by then we were completely plastered, and we rarely remembered much. From this point on in the night, all sorts of crazy things often happened. There is no question that I was definitely looking for love in all the wrong places.

It was on one of those nights out that I met a young woman. I have no recollection at all of the earlier portion of the evening, or the context of how we met. What I do remember is that I had met a woman, and toward the end of the night we had decided to take a walk up into the neighborhood behind the bar. San Francisco has many small parks and public spaces situated between rows and rows of housing, and we'd walked to one of them and sat down on a bench, just to keep talking, to keep the night going. There was definitely a sense of romance in the air.

My heart's desire, my deepest wish or goal in life, was not to meet Ms. Right Now, but to meet Ms. Right. Up until this time—I was around twenty-four years old—I'd never had a girlfriend, let alone met my soulmate. I had not yet been able to achieve my one and only ambition in life.

This particular night, I really liked this girl. We seemed to hit it off. She was attractive, nice, and seemed down to earth. She told me she was a buyer for The Gap, the clothing company based in San Francisco. I didn't know what a buyer did exactly, but it sounded pretty cool. I must have told her I was still in school, at USF, and that I planned to work for my family after graduation. It truly was a great night, with real promise. At the end of the night, I'm sure I took her phone number and told her I would be in touch soon.

Of course, I never called. I know how unkind that was. But I had so many internal issues, some of which are already apparent, and more of which will be revealed shortly. My intention was never to be unkind; I was simply protecting myself from some unknown dread. This was basically me, between the ages of eighteen and twenty-four. Tolerating school until the weekend, when I could drink, smoke, hang with friends and maybe meet a young woman. This was the way for me. Seven years of university down the drain.

Yes, I did eventually graduate, but to me that's beside the point.

TEN

P4BB*

*Because I will to know myself,
I see you as God's Son and my brother.*
—A Course in Miracles T-9.II.12:6

O KAY, one more drinking story. Guess I can't help myself.

When I was around nineteen years old, I was drinking some beers with my friends (shocker). By then, we had discovered the joys of alcohol, and would sneak some beers or wine here and there when there were no parents around. Note: it wasn't always beer and wine. For instance, my friend Chris' dad traveled often for work and he would collect those little liquor bottles you get on the airplane. On one occasion, we raided that garbage bag full of those little liquor bottles, which rested on the floor in his dad's closet, and we drank them and had a ball. But on this weekend, anyway, we were drinking some beers.

As I sipped my third or fourth beer in Chris' backyard, I randomly reviewed my young drinking "career."

By then, we'd had many alcohol-infused weekends and alcohol-related experiences; high school parties, weekends at Chris', or when my folks were away. Fairly typical. As I reviewed my experiences with alcohol, I recalled that on several occasions, I had had too much to drink and, in one form or another, made a total ass of myself. Or worse, I was cruel or mean to someone in some way I was not even aware of. On most occasions, though, we didn't overdrink too much and would end up having a great time. The one thing that I was keenly aware of as I sat there having this early life review was that drinking (as most people know) took away all my fear and sense of guilt. At least temporarily. Which is why I loved to drink so much. So the payoff was a seemingly deep sense of peace that came with the effects of alcohol. But drinking too much would, and occasionally did, lead to disaster.

I was thinking about all this loosely as I sipped my beer. Thinking about the range of drunkenness. One to three beers, you don't feel too much—perhaps a little buzz, but the world is still basically the same. Five to fifteen+ beers, and you, in short, can become an idiot. Say things you don't mean. Do things to others or yourself you completely regret. Ahh, but four beers. That, I noted as pondered these things, was the happy zone.

A perfect four-beer buzz. At four beers, I usually felt not just a buzz, but an *inner glow*. At four beers in, all my troubles — with relationships in my family, my insecurities and self-loathing related to my "lower" position in the pecking order of my rat pack of friends, underperforming academically at school, shyness around the girls I had a crush on, that never-ending sense of guilt—*all* that was behind me, or out of my mind, at four beers. At four beers in, I was a truly happy camper. It is a perfect buzz, low enough that I still have sense enough not to do anything stupid, but *high* enough that I could be my true self. At four beers in, I was, at least in my own mind, fearless, funny, part of the gang, comfortable, and free. My best qualities came out at four beers. Liquid confidence. Four beers. I loved a four-beer buzz.

And so sitting there in Chris' backyard drinking my beer, I thought, *wouldn't it be great if I could have a four-beer buzz all the time—a Permanent Four-Beer Buzz?* That would be ideal. I could be happy if I had a permanent four-beer buzz. Just think what life would be like then, free of fear and guilt … Hmmm.

I don't remember if I told Chris L., or Chris A., or Ben or Jon about this that day, or if I just kept it to myself. All I know is that it sounded like a really damn good idea to me at the time.

The Miracle of Forgiveness

Fast forward now about thirty years. I am fifty-one years old. I am standing in our lower barn on Rhinefarm, which is full of all kinds of tools and equipment, doing some work. I am cutting T-stakes (grapevine stakes) into twenty-eight-inch lengths with a band saw. We will be using these shortened stakes to fix broken grape stakes out in the vineyard. As I am working, Abel, our vineyard manager, walks into the barn. After a little chatting, he asks, "Hey Rob, would you be able to work on Sundays?" I paused, just for a moment, considered the request, and calmly said, "No." There were a variety of reasons why I didn't want to work Sundays. Abel smiled and said, "Yes, me neither." And that was the end of the conversation. It didn't take long after he left the barn for me to reflect on what a *miracle* I had just beheld.

By this time I had been a Course student for around fourteen years. The Course teaches its students that they have only one function while they are here on earth: to heal his or her mind. That is it. Plain and simple.

The world, by contrast, teaches us that we all have a thousand functions, and then a thousand more on top of that: go to school, get a job, pay the bills, eat less, be nice, drive the speed limit, write a book, fix the grape stake, be a good parent, play tennis, meditate, do yoga, etc.. Most of us occupy all our time fulfilling, or trying to fulfill, all these functions, while also solving the endless problems that result from our attempting to fulfill all these functions.

The Course says to its students, you only have one function: heal your mind. Because the mind is split into two, between Spirit (what the Course calls the Holy Spirit) and the ego. The goal is to undo the split, or heal the mind, and return the mind to Spirit. For Course students, this is accomplished in two ways: practicing a special form of forgiveness, and asking for and following the guidance of the Holy Spirit (Who will then guide the student to practice forgiveness). Anyway, I am a Course student, and so I have been devoted (as much as possible) to healing my mind for the past decade or so.

What is the result of all this? What is the result of practicing the Course's special form of forgiveness? (a process I describe in the appendix at the back of this book). What is the result of learning to follow the guidance of the Holy Spirit? A *Permanent Four-Beer Buzz!* With an asterisk. Okay, the buzz is not permanent (yet). But there is hope.

I guess what I am trying to say is that there is a way to get a *Permanent Four-Beer Buzz** without the alcohol and without all that guilt. This is not a judgement on alcohol or alcohol consumption, by the way. I know of many Course students, who don't have a drinking problem like me, who enjoy a glass of wine or beer on occasion. What I am saying is that the spiritual journey, in general, is a journey towards that *inner glow* that I mentioned with a four-beer buzz. It is possible to be "high" without booze! God Almighty, thank the Lord for that. I have found that when I am in my right mind (a Course term), I have that inner glow, or sense of peace naturally, without any outside influences (like beer or even a special relationship). The inner glow, or peace of mind, comes simply from my understanding and acceptance that I am one with God, right *now*, and will be forevermore. And the peace comes from knowing everyone else is, too, even if they are not aware of it (see quote at the top of this chapter). That is what the asterisk means: you get the *Permanent Four-Beer Buzz* — *without* the guilt, fear, and hangover. That is what the spiritual journey is ultimately for. That is its purpose. This is what I have learned as a student of the Course.

Does this mean I am always in a state of *Four-Beer Buzz* now? Ah, no. Case in point. Last weekend, my friends and I all got together for golf and Texas Hold 'em. We do this two or three times a year. The usual suspects were there: Ben, Chris, Eric, Len and Kurt. But this weekend, Arnie and Randy joined, too! It was a lot of fun, as usual.

Question: How do you know if you are spiritually enlightened or not? Answer: sit down and play Texas Hold 'em with your friends, that's how. See what happens. Ironically, I've noticed as I watch my mind while we are playing that I *lose* my *Four-Beer Buzz* (or am *out* of my right mind) when I am playing them all in poker. Why? Because I want to win, damn it! I want to take all their money and dominate. Needless to say, Spirit, or forgiveness, teaches the Course student to transcend concepts such as winning and losing, dominating or submitting, etc. Peace of mind comes from overlooking, and *being*, it teaches. And as a Course student, I try my darnedest during these poker sessions to watch my mind, heal my mind, overlook my impulse to win, and forgive the scene before me. But I just can't. I fail miserably. I gotta take down those pots!

This last weekend, for instance, I kept getting good cards, and good hands, but when I bet, someone always had a better hand. Or I would play a hand perfectly and still lose. And it pissed me off! (Not really, but kind of.)

For instance, I had a strong two pairs in my hand after the flop, and bet accordingly. I raised three dollars. A few stayed in, including Chris, and a few folded. So far so good. Then on the turn, I noted there were three spades on the board (meaning a possible flush opportunity for my opponents), and so it was time to get serious and push everyone out of the pot. So I bet eight dollars—a fairly big bet in our home game—and everyone folded, as they should have ... except Chris. Chris proceeded to call my big bet, even though he had no business being in that hand—I had put him on a flush draw. Sure enough, a spade turned over on the river, and I already knew I'd lost (Chris did hit his flush).

That is how my whole poker weekend was going. Not long after Chris crushed me, I was down nearly $150, which means I was maxed out and ready to quit and go watch March Madness on the couch. Did I have my Four-Beer Buzz on? Ah, no. I was a little annoyed. But it is true that I was having fun, of course. I love playing poker with my friends, not just for the games and camaraderie, but also because it gives me an opportunity to see how far I've come on the spiritual journey. Clearly, after this weekend, I have a ways to go. The day I am truly joyful and happy inwardly when my fives over aces full boat gets cracked by an aces over fives full boat will signal that I have arrived home in God.

Anyways, though I have not yet achieved my goal of peace of mind, or what the Course would call "healed my mind wholly," I have come a long way. While my Four-Beer buzz is not *permanent* yet, I still get a forgiveness buzz quite often. Take the scene in the barn from above. Abel asked me to work on Sundays. I said no. Simple enough, right? But not so fast.

After Abel left the barn, after asking me about working Sundays, I continued to work with a happy and deeply grateful "buzz," for I recognized the miracle. This was a great example of my shift to asking Spirit for guidance and thinking with the Spirit, instead of thinking with and acting with the ego.

In my youth, before the age of twenty-six, before The Plunge and before learning of Spirit and following Its guidance, this is how it would have went (and actually did—so many other times). Abel would have asked me to work on Sundays, and in a flash, my ego would have told me the following story (mostly in my unconscious mind):

"Abel is an authority over you. You are nothing. But if you say yes and work for Abel on Sundays, you will get Abel's approval, and maybe then you will be something. He will like you. You will have his approval. Then you will be saved. Only if you please him, will you be saved (Push down and deny your heart's wish *not* to work on Sundays. That means nothing. It's not about you. Forget about it!)"

Then, deeper still in the unconscious mind, the ego

says, "You are a victim of Abel 'making' you work on Sundays, so now you can hate him for asking you to do it. But *deny* this hate and push it *deep* into the unconscious, because it would violate your belief that you are 'holier than thou' and are nice and please others."

And so, had Abel asked me if I could work on Sundays before all my healing and the spiritual journey, I would have said, "Yes! No problem, Abel!" How many times in my youth did I say Yes when I meant No, and said No when I meant Yes? And accept all the attendant inner rage and self-loathing to go along with it? God only knows. Enough, I suppose, that I finally cracked, and fell into The Plunge.

I didn't mean to get all dark here, but I guess if I write about the ego, it's gotta go that way.

The point of this chapter is that I have learned, at last, and mercifully, that a *Permanent Four-Beer Buzz** is possible. Amen. It comes, in my case, from asking the Holy Spirit for guidance, asking Him to decide for God for me. It comes with the miracle of forgiveness that the Course teaches. It comes with love. Love for myself. Love for my brother, who is the Son of God. And love for God Himself, my Creator. Other spiritual paths will have other terms, ideas, and practices, but the goal will always be the same: a *Permanent Four-Beer Buzz** (or the peace of God). Amen.

ELEVEN

A Wild Gun Bun
National Sales Manager

O F COURSE, the drinking didn't end when I left college. In fact, I used to tell people that drinking in college was like the minor leagues compared to the drinking I would do working for the winery. That was the Majors.

After college, at the tender age of twenty-four, I was hired by Dad as the national sales manager for Gundlach Bundschu. I would travel the country, presenting our wines to hundreds of customers and working with our national distributors to promote our wines. Youth, travel, restaurants, bars, nightlife—to many, this job may have seemed to be an ideal one for me. And I thought it was. But as it turned out, the job would end up being my undoing.

A typical day on the road (sales trip) went like this: wake up in the morning with a big hangover, dress in coat and tie or business casual, get picked up by a distributor rep at my hotel around nine a.m., and we'd do a ride-along for the day, making what essentially amounted to sales calls. The cities varied, and I could be anywhere, like St. Louis or Charlotte.

In the wine business, the supplier rep (me, representing Gun Bun) and a local distributor rep (representing our wine distributor in a local market) get together and drive around to key wine accounts where Gun Bun is served, or where the local rep would like to place Gun Bun in a new account. We would arrive at a wine shop, supermarket, or restaurant, and meet the buyer to talk wine, and hopefully make a placement (sale).

By the time lunch rolled around, we'd typically end up eating at a restaurant that served our wine. Of course I'd pop a bottle for the meal—gotta keep checking quality standards and all. Perhaps after lunch, I might do a wine presentation to the restaurant server staff. Then in the afternoon, off to call on more accounts.

All this time, I'm sampling our wine with each buyer at each account—instead of spitting. Normally at each account, it's customary for the tasters—often the sales rep and the buyer—to spit out the wine into a container designed specifically for that purpose, in order to prevent inebriation. But I didn't spit. Why? Because I wanted— needed—to drink, just to alleviate the huge anxiety I felt while doing all this. By the end of the afternoon, I'd already be three-quarters of the way in the tank.

But the day's not over! I might have a wine dinner to host that night—with lots more wine, maybe some port and cigars at the end of the night. Crash in bed.

Wake up hungover the next morning. Rinse. Repeat.

Occasionally, on some of the more wild nights, I would meet a girl.

And that was life on the road. Typically, sales trips lasted two weeks before I would come crawling back home to my own bed. Externally, for awhile, everything seemed to be going fine. Gun Bun made its sales. The world kept turning. And I kept my head above water. Barely. But what I never shared with anyone, mostly because I was hardly aware of it myself, was that the job created an extraordinary amount of stress and anxiety.

There was a massive chasm between my job and my inner world. The fact is, my job terrified me. People terrified me. Sales calls terrified me. Public speaking *really* terrified me. But I did it all, all day, every day, as the national sales manager. I would take that fear and just stuff it down inside me, brush it out of the way, and carry on. Hear no evil. See no evil. Speak no evil. The truth was, my happy-go-lucky, outgoing personality was just a mask. Deep down, I was a deeply shy, introverted person, with titanically low self-esteem and self-worth, faking it all the way.

I was so uncomfortable around people that I couldn't look anyone in the eye when I spoke to them. Any strong personality intimidated me. Over the years, I had worked out a habit wherein I would focus on a point between someone's eyes, so that I would give them the impression that I was looking them in the eye. But I never was.

I could go on and on, but I think I've made my point—

I think I can finally close the case that I had severe issues. And they were all rising to the surface on the job. Yet I repressed all this dark stuff and kept it at bay with drink and movement.

I lasted for about two years as our national sales manager.

(Recently, my friend Eric reminisced about my lack of confidence in those days, while he also observed how much I have changed since then for the better.)

And so into this cauldron of inner turmoil and deep emotional and physical stress I was experiencing working as national sales manager, came the next event, the one that would finally do me in: I fell in love for the first time.

I have been referencing a personal "fall" of a sort over and over again ("The Plunge"), and we have reached the point where I think it's time to share this story. This event is one of two central experiences in my life that have inspired me to write this book. It is the event that kicked me out my sleeping, material-oriented mind—my normal life—and launched me on my spiritual journey. I am pausing here to share this, because I have to say that the following story is going to take a massive turn "out into left field."

So far, I hope I have conveyed a relatively normal life with normal events. Yes, too much drinking and internal issues, but these are of course common around the world. But overall, I've not shared anything extraordinary. Until now. The story I am going to share really happened, and I will describe it as best I can. I have shared this experience with others only a handful of times, to a couple of therapists and a few people close to me. You'll understand why I never bring it up in polite conversation. This story is the pivotal point of my life; it's what changed everything.

This is what happened.

TWELVE

Falling Madly in Love

IT'S EARLY May of 1997, I'm twenty-six years old, and I am standing at a pay phone in baggage claim at SFO, waiting for my luggage to arrive, and also waiting for my newish girlfriend to answer her phone. That's right: my dream had finally come true. About three months earlier, I had gone out to dinner on a first date with a lovely young woman, and I was head-over-heels by the time they cleared the appetizer plate. Shockingly, a follow-up call after the date revealed that she had good feelings, too, and a second date was made.

The experience of falling in love turned out to be everything the movies, books, poetry, etc. had been alluding to for years. Blissful, euphoric, exciting, and a sense that I had at last found what I'd been looking for. Anyway, it was her — "the one" — whom I was calling at the airport.

Two weeks earlier, I had left for what would be one hell of a sales trip. This time I passed through New Mexico and southern California, meeting with distributor partners, making sales calls, and doing the general routine.

But on this particular trip, I was deeply agitated inside and barely present with any of the folks I was meeting. The reason was that along with the usual stress of just performing my job, a little spot of fear had recently begun to creep into my mind. In short, I had found Shangri-La at last—and then the thought that I could lose it, or, to be more specific, *her*, began to take over my mind. *She could leave me.* This idea had taken form, and then like a tumor, it began to grow and fester in my mind until my mind began to spin.

Thus, on this sales trip, while externally doing my job, inwardly, most of my time was spent in my mind, analyzing phone conversations with her, trying to read into things. Did she even miss me? Doubt, anxiety, fear— all the gobbledygook of my lifetime of self-doubt, every negative thought or emotion I'd ever repressed in the past, was churning to the surface on this trip. Of course, I drank tons, trying to keep the darkness at bay. But that only made it worse. My long career of drinking and repression seemed to be finally taking its toll. Picture a teapot just as it's approaching the boiling point.

As if to put an exclamation mark on this trip, on the way to the airport in New Mexico from where I'd be heading to L.A., I got into a fender bender in my rental car, driving my stress level even higher. Needless to say, I was having a rough sales trip.

Sometime in the middle of this trip, my girlfriend and I had made plans over the phone for her to borrow her roommate's car and pick me up at SFO when I returned home. The plan was for me to stay the night at her apartment in the City.

When I landed at SFO after another jittery week in L.A., my anxiety had risen even higher. And I also had a slight buzz, because it was so clear I was having a rough day that the flight attendant on the way up from L.A. offed me a couple of complimentary little drink bottles.

The main reason for my upset was that I had not spoken to her since the day we'd made pick-up arrangements, which was a few days earlier, and somehow I seemed to know something was amiss. Sure enough, after we landed and I got off the plane, she was nowhere to be seen. My underlying anxiety now ramped up to the point where I was *really* upset. That's when I went over to the pay phone at baggage claim and called her to see where she was.

She picked up. I was really spinning and full of emotion now, but I asked as nicely and calmly as I could, "Why aren't you here?"

She calmly told me, "I wasn't able to borrow the car after all." And then silence. No apologies, or a friendly, "Grab a cab and come over!" Just a dead silence.

I stood there stunned, not knowing what to say. After a couple of ticks, I quietly said, "I have to go." And then I hung up the phone.

Without getting into the weeds of this relationship, I'll just translate what this—all my doubts and fears culminating into this one phone conversation—meant in my mind: *She doesn't love me.* I was devastated.

Later, I would learn that this belief wasn't necessarily so, but by then I was already well on my way to losing it. This airport incident was the spark that would ignite what came next.

Talk about "leaving your heart in San Francisco."

THIRTEEN

A Plunge into Hell

Aᴏᴛᴇʀ I hung up the phone, I collected my bags and then made the harrowing journey back to Sonoma —over an hour-long bus trip, then a transfer to a taxi in Petaluma, a neighboring town. My roommates had thrown a big party that Saturday night, and when I got home, the house was completely empty and also completely trashed. There were wine and beer bottles scattered all over the place. I eventually found everyone downtown, where I joined them and began to drink in earnest. I would end up drinking to blackout that night, something I was beginning to do more and more often. All the while, inwardly I was still devastated, and my anxiety level was actually creeping even higher.

The following Monday, I went into work on Rhinefarm, but I was not all right. In fact, I was so disturbed that I met with Dad and asked him if it would be okay to take the day off—something I'd never done—because "I had some things I needed to figure out."

He agreed, and I went home, turned on some music, sat on the floor, and began to ruminate about my relationship.

What is going wrong? Why hasn't she called? (We still hadn't spoken since the airport.) *Is it over? What is love anyway? What are all these feelings coming up?* Question after question sprung to my mind, while I sat there hour after hour. And it didn't stop on Monday. I took the next four days off and just stayed home, again listening to music, sitting on the living room floor, my mind just spinning and spinning, getting more and more lost in thought.

At the same time, over each of those four nights, I could not get to sleep. Literally not a wink. I tried everything, including my old tricks. NyQuil the first night; sleeping pills the next. But my mind was now spinning so fast, and the fear and anxiety level was so high, that sleep would not come no matter what I did. I'm also not sure I ate much, if anything, over those four days.

I think AJ and Mike, my friends and roommates, knew something was wrong, but they gave me my space. No one, including me as it turns out, was aware of the fact that I was actually in the process of losing my mind.

By the fifth day, I could barely keep it together. Unable to sit longer, I started driving. I drove to the City and probably passed by her apartment. Then the idea hit me—I don't know why or how—that I was going to die. So I drove down to Ocean Beach and parked the car and waited to die. I sat there for a few minutes and then decided maybe I wasn't going to die. I then drove the hour trip north, back up to Sonoma, drove around a little more, and by then, evening had come.

Things had gotten extremely dire. My mind was

spinning so fast that I literally could not stop all these random thoughts from spinning through my mind at a maddening pace, and what had been anxiety before was now raw fear. Getting the sense that I was going to crack, in a state of pure panic, I drove over to Dad and Nancy's house to ask for help. It had occurred to me that if I didn't get to sleep soon, I might lose it forever. I was truly on the brink.

It turns out they were having a dinner party and Jeff was there, too, along with some guests. I asked them—Dad and Jeff—to step outside, where I tried to explain what was going on. They did their best to try to calm me down, but by now it was too late. I was begging them to take me to the emergency room so a doctor could give me some drugs to knock me out. Though the conversation probably lasted about five minutes, inwardly it felt like an hour or more. I felt deeply frustrated trying to make my point that my mental state had hit the fan.

It took much convincing, but in the end they finally clued in that I was in deep trouble, and they agreed to take me down to the Sonoma Valley Hospital emergency room.

It was Thursday evening, May 15, 1997, probably around six p.m. I know this because around twenty years later, I returned to the hospital and asked them to check the records for me.

By the time we arrived at the emergency room, I was already halfway gone. At some point along the way, all the fear and mind spinning had suddenly stopped. I was now in a sort of strange, quiet state, where everything seemed as if it was moving in slow motion. The receptionist in the waiting area asked me to sign myself in while Dad and Jeff stood by, behind me. I could barely write down my name. My vision had become distorted and everything was in a kind of fog. The receptionist then asked me to come through a door against the back wall and around through the back, into the patient care area, where the doctor could have a look at me.

Looking back, it was after I followed the receptionist's directions and passed through the door and back to the patient care room, that I slipped into an hallucination. I wasn't aware I had done so, but as I headed back towards the patient care area, I found myself in what I can only describe as an alternate reality.

I was no longer afraid at all. All that fear and anxiety had just up and disappeared. In fact, it had been replaced by a deep, quiet stillness. I had, without realizing it, just become an observer.

The first thing I did was ask someone if I could go to the bathroom. And so I did. I found myself looking at my reflection in the mirror in the bathroom, and it was really amazing. My eyes, which are usually fairly narrow in shape, were big and round and wide open. And I remember looking into them and seeing an almost-glow in my eyes, somewhat like a gentle light. I was startled, because I had never seen my eyes look like that. After a moment, I left the bathroom and headed back toward the patient care area, having not bothered to actually use a toilet.

If it hadn't already done so, this is when everything truly took a turn for the surreal. To my left, as I walked, I observed shelves stacked to the ceiling with cardboard boxes. I remember vaguely thinking it was an odd sight to see in an emergency room. The lighting in the room was not the typical bright florescent light of a hospital, but rather dark, with shadows lurking in the corners— the kind of lighting you see in the basement scene of a horror movie. It was unclear where the dim light was coming from, another oddity. I didn't think anything about it, though, as again I was in a quiet "observer" state of mind.

After a few steps down a hall, I turned the corner into the patient care area. It was like no patient care area I'd ever seen or heard of. Standing a little distance off to my right was the doctor, but now he was a vague figure who was not looking at me at all, but kind of standing erect and still and looking in a direction away from me, to my right. I turned to start walking towards him, and as I did, I passed by a single chair to my left. I glanced at it as I walk by. It was no typical patient care bed. In fact, it was a dental chair, turquoise, angled and sitting there ominously.

The whole room was now dark, except this chair, which was somehow in the light. I quickly glanced at the larger-than-normal tray where the dentist puts his tools—just to the right of the chair. But rather than the little dental tools, this tray was loaded with the most sinister of instruments, much larger and more exaggerated tools, that could only be used for torture. A big saw, a giant hook, a meat cleaver and other instruments that were designed to be used for the most heinous of intentions. Oddly enough, I did not react at all to what I was seeing. And I was still wholly unaware that I was in the middle of an hallucination, in the middle of a living nightmare.

I arrived in front of the doctor and was standing before him. He looked like a doctor, with the white lab coat and all. He had dark hair and a goatee. But all of these details quickly faded into the background, because I was focused solely on his eyes. I didn't know what I was looking at, but I was not looking into the eyes of a man. They were silvery and sparkling, and both eyes were spinning clockwise, like nothing I've ever seen. And there was a look of *pure evil* and a seething hatred in them that was so deep and so profound that I would never be able to translate it into words. It was as if all the evil contained in all the universe throughout all time had contracted like a black hole into two points—those steely eyes. It clearly wanted to murder me.

But there I was, deer in those headlights, still quiet, looking, having no clue what was going on really, just gazing into those eyes which seemed to run as deep as the universe itself, a bottomless pit.

Then, zap! For lack of better words, my mind, or awareness, or very being, was suddenly *sucked* straight into those eyes! I literally had the experience of being sucked into those eyes, like light gets sucked into a black hole. And I found myself in a void. I was in a limitless, lifeless void where there was literally nothing.

Nothing. No light or dark, no hospital or (evil) doctor, no dental chair, no Sonoma, no color, no pain or pleasure, no thought, no emotion, no form of any kind, no me, either. Nothing. Or Nothingness. The only thing there, it seems, was an observer, observing it all.

I would spend many years trying to make sense of this moment. I seemed literally to have left the world and gone to Nowhere. This state of nothingness, or *i am nothing*, only lasted a moment or two, and then—zap!— just as quickly, I was pulled out of that empty state, back through those eyes, and I was standing in this darkened room once again, standing before this evil creature, staring into those sinister eyes.

But everything changed. Suddenly, finally, I was acutely aware that I was in deep, deep trouble. I had finally awoken to the fact that all's not right in Kansas. I was in a state of perfect terror. I don't mean afraid, or anxious, or even terrified. I mean I was literally frozen, in a state of what I can only describe as perfect, complete, unmitigated *terror*. I couldn't imagine anyone ever having an experience of such an intense state of terror as I was experiencing right now. I was frozen before this thing, and I didn't know what to do, or even where I was. Years later, I would secretly pat myself on the back because I didn't piss my pants in this moment.

And now we have arrived at what I'll call my third mystical experience. For the first time in my life, I would receive spiritual guidance. I would not have described it that way standing there, frozen in horror. And in fact, I would not describe it that way for many years to come. My comment at the beginning of this book made it clear that I didn't have a "spiritual" bone in my body. But without a doubt, I would receive my first communication from a Voice or Presence from beyond this world, right there, right then, while I was frozen in horror in that godforsaken underworld in front of that godforsaken thing.

Still unable to move, or think, or even breathe, terrified beyond measure—which sounds as if I'm being melodramatic, but it was really that bad—standing before that thing, a Thought emerged in my mind that clearly did not come from me. It is the first time and the last time that I have ever experienced a thought that seemed to come from elsewhere, outside my mind. It was as if a loving parent quietly whispered straight into my mind what to do.

The Voice said, "Run."

Still frozen, I heard this idea, and suddenly there was nothing more I wanted to do but to escape from this place. My guidance was to run, but how? To where? For a split second, I didn't know.

Then, somehow, the facts of the situation became clear in my mind. It occurred to me that I must be in two places at once. Intuitively, I suddenly understood that behind this darkened room, behind this Devil, behind this hallucination before me, I must still actually have been in the Sonoma Valley Hospital emergency room, and I must actually have been standing before a real, normal doctor. I could not perceive the hospital or the doctor in his normal human form, but I understood it all must be there, just beyond my perception. So a plan of escape began to form in my mind.

I cannot overstate how much I wanted to get away from this place. There was nothing in my life I have ever wanted more—not even a girlfriend. But there was also a deep fear that I would fail, and that I would be stuck here forever. I was truly and completely terrified.

I tried getting a grip on the situation. I considered just turning around and running, as the Voice said. But it occurred to me that if I did so, I would never escape that emergency room. Either the (evil) doctor would stop me, or Dad and Jeff (who of course had absolutely no idea what I was going through) would catch me on the way out. So that wouldn't work. And then suddenly another plan took shape in my mind: I would deceive *it*.

This is the critical moment of the story. I was still standing in front of this thing, staring straight into its swirling eyes. I was still in a peak state of terror. My plan was to ask the doctor—who I now believed was "behind" this (evil) doctor before me—if I could go talk to my dad and brother for a moment. This was not my real intent. My real intent was to get the hell out of Dodge—to run. But I had to escape from Hell first. *Everything* in this moment was riding on what the (evil) doctor/doctor would say.

So I began to try to speak, to ask my question. But my

mouth was full of cotton balls; it was completely dry, and for a moment I literally could not talk. I swallowed once or twice to try to clear my throat. And then I tried again. I was in a state of sheer desperation, and terrified that the doctor will say no. *What will happen to me?* It was not a peak experience but the opposite, a valley experience. Maybe as in the Valley of Death?

And so I cleared my throat again, and then somehow, very quietly and with a cracked little voice, I was able to get out the words, "Can I go talk to my dad and brother for a moment?"

There was the briefest of pauses. Time seemed to freeze. Everything in the hallucination froze except for those sparkling eyes, which continued to ominously rotate clockwise. Then I could see its lips move, and its answer was muffled and unclear. But it was clear enough that I understood that the doctor said, "Yes" to my question, and for the first time in what seemed like forever, something besides terror entered my world—a glimmer of hope.

Heart racing, as slowly and as calmly as I could, I turned from the (evil) doctor (I was still in Hell), and started to walk back through the darkened room, past the dental chair, through the hallway, and towards the door that led back into the waiting area where Jeff and Dad were waiting. Looking back, it was somewhere on that short walk that I transitioned out of the hallucination and back into this world.

Hope was now really beginning to fill me, but I knew

I was not out of the woods yet. For I knew there was no way Dad and Jeff would let me leave this emergency room. It's understandable, of course; I'd gone half-mad in their eyes. I needed help. And I was the one who asked them to bring me here in the first place.

The original plan was to get me drugs so I could sleep. They also obviously would have no clue what I just experienced, and so I knew intuitively that they would not let me go. And there, again, was the knowledge that there was literally nothing I have ever wanted more than to escape that hospital in that moment.

And so I walked through the door in the back of the waiting room, and there were Jeff and Dad, standing there looking at me. I was never so happy to see them, but this was no time for reunions. For there, beyond them, on the opposite side of the room, were the glass exit doors, which led outside, into a Sonoma neighborhood and the free world beyond.

Without hesitation, I just lowered my shoulder like an NFL running back and charged. I bulled right into and through them as they tried to grab me and stop me. Many years later, I asked Dad what he remembered about this moment.

He said, "It was amazing. You ran at us, and we both got hold of you at first. I got a solid hold of you myself (Dad is naturally a strong guy). But you just flicked me off of you like I was nothing! I couldn't believe it."

It seems I was given a superhuman strength in that moment, because I did escape their grasp. All of this is a blur in my memory, but I made it through to the other side, and out the door into the night! I'd never felt such relief and gratitude as I did when I ran away from that emergency room. I was free.

Close to two weeks later, I would find myself on a couch, recounting this story to a new psychotherapist with whom I'd be working for the next fifteen years. I used words like "hell" and "the Devil" and "Satan" to describe what I had experienced, because really, what other descriptors are out there that would adequately describe what I encountered? And I gave the experience a name that day on the couch, which I have referred to in my mind ever since. I called it "The Plunge."

Thankfully the therapist reassured me in those first days of therapy that it was all an hallucination, that I did not in fact go to hell, and that this kind of thing is common in the world. It was just what I needed to hear, and it gave me a little comfort.

Of course, I would be shell-shocked for quite some time to come, and it would be many years before I could say I was able to let go of the lingering fear that stayed with me since that night.

In fact, I'm not sure I have succeeded yet.

FOURTEEN

Napa Road

A FTER I escaped the emergency room, I ran down the street into the cool night air. Not sure where to go, there was one thing I *was* sure of: I did not want Dad and Jeff to find me and take me back to the emergency room.

About two blocks from the hospital, I came upon a little bridge that spanned across a small creek running parallel to the street. The creek was mostly dry, so I dashed down under the bridge and hid. I lay curled in the fetal position for I don't know how long, shivering, but just happy to be back in the world. Sometime early in the morning, after I was sure they weren't around, I crawled out from under the bridge and made the fifteen-minute walk back home to Club 590 (that's what my friends Mike and AJ and I loved to call our party house, located on 590 Harris Road).

I was still sleepless later that morning when Dad, who maybe had also gone sleepless, came over to our house, picked me up, and took me back up to his house. Presumably, they were trying to figure out what to do with me.

Meanwhile, I sat on the couch in their living room, pretending to flip through a magazine, as both Jeff and Katie, who were there presumably to check on me, sat nearby. What was really happening was that my mind was now completely out of control, with random thoughts just swirling about. I was merely an observer of these thoughts, which were separate from me, apparently coming from a mysterious independent source. They came and went so fast that I literally couldn't keep up with them. It was now Friday morning; I hadn't slept since the previous Saturday night. To say the experience was deeply frightening and uncomfortable is a gross understatement.

Suddenly, while I was still sitting there on the couch, a thought came up that literally stopped the hyper-spinning thought stream and silenced my mind: *I am Jesus and I must die for their sins.*

Yes, that was a crazy thought, but not a surprising one, because I *was* losing my mind. I roughly remember the logic that led to that insane thought. While sitting there, reviewing the previous night in the emergency room, it occurred to me, *That experience was so deep and dark and awful, God —if there is a God—would not have asked a regular person to go through it. Kinda like what happened to Jesus on the cross. Therefore, I must be Jesus!* It made sense to me in that moment, and then the thought, so long taught in Christianity, "...I must die for their sins," came next. Unfortunately, I was off my rocker by now, and so I took the thought literally.

I stood up from the couch, turned to Jeff and Katie, and told them I loved them. Then I turned and walked out the front door of the house and began to run down the driveway towards Napa Road, which is a little over a hundred yards below the house. Full of adrenaline and fear, but determined, I ran down the road, which winds between a block of Cabernet grapes and an open pasture. When I got to the shoulder of Napa Road, a 55-mph two-lane highway that runs between Sonoma and Napa, I waited for a split second until I saw a white car approaching from my left around a bend, and then I just ran out into the middle of the road and raised my hands. Madly, I had decided to take my own life, in order to "...die for their sins." The ironic thing was that I was not even a Christian and never believed in that teaching!

Well, my recollection gets pretty blurry from here. My emotions were through the roof, and the whole world seemed to slow down and take on a surreal nature. At the last instant, as the white car rushed towards me, I decided that maybe this wasn't such a good idea. And so I began to dive off to my left, towards a ditch that ran along the side of the road adjacent to the vineyard and my parents' house. I vaguely remember there was contact between me and the car.

The next thing I remember is crossing Napa Road from the *opposite* side (!?) and walking back to and up the driveway with Jeff, who had followed me out the door when I'd originally made my dash. Now, if you think there is a missing link in logic here, you'd be right. There is less logic to it than anything else that happened that day. What happened in between, I have no idea.

There was a part of me that had—and still has—the feeling that I died on Napa Road that day, and then returned into some sort of parallel universe, where everything appeared the same, but nothing *was* the same. It has given me a strange sort of insight, and I would argue that this is where my real spiritual journey began. Obviously, not too much happened in the physical universe, since I ended up with no physical injuries and I am still here to write about it. But what it feels like is that maybe I left some sort of wrong-minded existence on one side of the road, and began to come into my right mind on the other side of the road. And from there my life has continued, with a more spiritual and more expansive view of life.

Needless to say, this little incident on Napa Road probably brought on my family's decision as to what to do with me. Minutes after Napa Road, I was loaded into the back of our family Suburban. Then, Dad and Jeff drove me up to Santa Rosa, a neighboring city about forty minutes away, to a hospital. When we got there, they walked me to the psychiatric wing of the hospital, where, amazingly, I was able to check myself in voluntarily. I must have looked like a zombie, but I was still just barely able to write.

I don't remember anything after that, until I woke up approximately two days later, in a bed, in the psychiatric ward of the hospital.

God Almighty, I was finally able to get to sleep. And

God Almighty, my life changed dramatically from this point forward.

FIFTEEN

First Prayer

MY LONG recovery from The Plunge began with ten days in the hospital. Sometime on or about the third night, I found myself in bed, once again unable to sleep. It was late, and the fear that I might return to the hallucination began to bubble up. In an act of desperation, I got up from my bed and walked down to the nursing station, where I asked if I could try to sleep on the couch in the community room. There was a TV in there, and in my life, the TV has always been a useful tool to help me get to sleep, because it distracts me from my spinning thoughts. Thankfully, they agreed.

After the TV was turned on, I curled up on the couch and tried to sleep. The TV was playing *Star Trek*, one of my all-time favorite shows. In the episode on this night, however, everyone on the bridge of the Enterprise, including Spock, was laughing hysterically. Since I knew Spock, a Vulcan, doesn't usually show emotions, I began to internally freak out there on the couch. "Oh my God, I'm hallucinating again! I haven't actually left the emergency room…" Once again, frightening thoughts began to spin through my mind. And so, for the very first time, I did something I had never done before: I prayed.

I closed my eyes and I prayed, "God, if You really exist, please give me peace of mind. All I want in the world is peace of mind. Please stop my mind from spinning so I can go to sleep. Please calm me down. Please, God."

Now, I didn't necessarily believe in God as I prayed, and it did feel a bit awkward, but as they say, *There are no atheists in foxholes.* Then, in my mind's eye, I visualized a Big Hand, light and benevolent, gently coming down on top of me as I lay curled there on the couch in the common room.

Amazingly, shortly after I made this prayer, it was answered. I swear I felt the temperature increase as I lay there visualizing the hand covering me (it was chilly in there), and soon, I became more comfortable. Then, my mind gently slowed down, and within a minute or two, I fell fast asleep. Years later I would marvel at this, because I was a semi-insomniac. It usually took me thirty minutes or longer to fall asleep. But that night, after the prayer, it was just a moment or two before I fell into a sweet sleep. I awoke a little while later and returned to my room and continued to sleep. For many years to come, sleep would be a very important thing to me.

More than twenty years later, I would learn that praying for peace of mind was a much bigger thing than I originally realized. That night, I just wanted a quiet mind so I could sleep. But what I later learned is that quieting the mind and joining with the light within is the way to lasting peace and healing. It is what mystics around the world have practiced for as long as anyone can remember.

From this experience, I would learn of the inherent power of the human mind, something not commonly taught in school or universities. You will understand as my story progresses why I believe that the mind, and what happens in the mind, is the whole ballgame when it comes to the spiritual journey. To quote one of my favorite movies for spiritual lessons, *Vanilla Sky*: "The subconscious [mind] is a very powerful thing."

SIXTEEN

Year on The Hill

OON AFTER my release from the hospital, I would lose
my position as national sales manager of the winery (shocker). I wasn't fired, though. Dad and Jeff
wisely sat me down in the living room of Mary's House
and asked me if I thought I was capable of continuing to
do my job. Everyone in the room, including me, knew the
answer to that one, and so I said, "No." And that was the
end of that.

And my girlfriend broke up with me. No big drama.
It was done quietly, over the phone. And, given all the
power and energy I had put into this relationship in terms
of my life's dream-come-true, you'd think I would've
been devastated when this happened. But actually, The
Plunge was so brutal, and I was so raw, that the breakup
barely registered. I clearly had other things on my mind.

At work, I moved back into the vineyard, where I had
worked growing up. I was given the project of clearing
the side of Arrowhead Mountain, which stretches just behind and adjacent to the winery, in order to plant a new
vineyard. Over the course of the fall of 1997 to the spring

of 1998, I led a team of six men as we clear-cut a bunch of oak trees in order to plant what is today one of our prized Cab vineyards, though there are other varietals up there as well, such as Malbec. All the while, I was going to therapy. Though it was a long and difficult job, one special thing did happen up there on "The Hill." On a cool, damp winter morning as I was trudging down the hill in mud and wet grass, I encountered a big, beautiful white owl quietly sitting on a branch of one of those oaks, not ten feet above me. It was a powerful moment for me. We stood and stared at each other for a few minutes. I felt deeply sad that I would be chopping down her home soon, and I hoped she would find a new one. Years later, I would learn that the owl has a lot of mystical symbolism associated with it. The owl has been associated with the divine, and in particular the divine feminine and the Goddess. In all my years of growing up and working on the ranch, I'd never seen an owl like this. She was truly majestic.

What's really cool is that we eventually created an exclusive wine club hat featuring a white owl above the bill. Of course I have one now and wear it proudly as I give tours. Technically, it was a coincidence that Therese, our amazing merchandise manager, designed these hats with the owl. But I no longer really believe in coincidences.

Another interesting thing that happened at this time is that there had apparently been some sort of shift in my mind. I call it an *opening*. Shortly after The Plunge, one day I went to the local Sonoma bookshop. I loved books and loved to read. On that day, I didn't have a particular book in mind, I just went to browse. Usually I gravitated over to the sci-fi section to see if there was an Orson Scott Card title I hadn't read, or maybe over to fiction to find the new Tom Clancy thriller.

But not this day. I was walking past a table full of books and I looked down, and there on the table was a book on angels. "Angels," "Spirituality," etc…, these types of books had been so far off my radar that I didn't even know they existed. But here was a little book on angels, and it just *called* to me. I bought it on a whim and took it home with me.

In those first days after The Plunge, I often just sat on my bed and paged through this new angel book. I don't remember much about the details of the book, other than that the writer clearly believed in the reality of angels. But it gave me great comfort. The idea of a "light" side to existence that could counterbalance the dark side I had just experienced really resonated with me. So I loved that angel book, and I looked at it often.

Keep in mind that I didn't all at once begin to believe in angels; I didn't lose my critical mind. Generally speaking, *If it doesn't make sense to me, I dismiss it,* was always my philosophy. This is why, over the years, as badly as I wanted at times to become a Christian, I simply couldn't do it. Because "Jesus sacrificed himself for my sins" never made any sense to me. And so I couldn't "give myself to Jesus," as Christianity asks. Anyway, with the angel book, I wasn't necessarily a believer, or a "born again" so to speak, but I did gently accept the idea of angels. They were a comforting idea in those early days after The Plunge. It would not be until around ten years later that I would really begin to dive deeply into spirituality. Getting this little angel book was a wonderful start.

At the end of my year during which we had successfully cleared the hill in preparation for planting grapevines, I ended up having another manic episode (which is what the doctors called The Plunge), after I had decided to quit taking meds because I so badly wanted to be "normal" again. It occurred shortly after I made the most epic, most difficult, scary decision I'd ever made. I had decided to quit the winery.

I just marched right into the kitchen of Mary's House early one morning while Dad and Grandma (Mary) were sitting there having their usual morning coffee, and I said, "I quit." And then I turned right around and marched out the door, and then had my second dip into madness.

Though this one was also deeply scary and uncomfortable, it was nothing compared to The Plunge. In the end, I ended up in the hospital again. After recovering to a degree from this episode, I'd had enough. The lifelong sense of guilt I'd always been saddled with was gone, and it was replaced now with an overwhelming sense of shame. In my own judgement, I was no longer a "normal" person. I was damaged goods, deeply flawed and generally, again in my own judgement, did not belong with normal society.

So one day in the fall of 1998, after taking a solo back-packing trip through Europe that summer (amazingly my therapist had cleared me for this trip with my family), I up and decided to move to L.A. to write the great American screenplay. I decided to get the hell out of Dodge, and nothing felt so right in my life. I knew nothing about Hollywood or screenplays and had never really dreamed about writing a screenplay before, but by God, that was what I was going to do. And so I packed my stuff and moved to L.A.

SEVENTEEN

L.A.

A s it turns out, I did not write the great American screenplay after all. I drove down to L.A., found an apartment in Redondo Beach, a small beach community located just south of L.A., and settled in. Having nothing to do—besides drinking and watching movies—I did eventually sit down to try to write the screenplay. I got as far as writing a treatment, which is a synopsis of a movie idea, and I submitted it to The Writers Guild in L.A. This is what screenwriters do to copyright, or protect, their movie idea, so no one can steal it when they go out to pitch the idea to film industry movers and shakers.

My movie, called *The Prize*, was set in the future. Loosely based on *Star Wars* and my love of sci-fi, it was about a farm boy who had to join in a global war game— aka a futuristic Super Bowl—where contestants fight to the death (similar to *The Hunger Games*) in order to save the girl. After I submitted the treatment, I never could sit down to write the screenplay itself. I just didn't have the confidence in myself.

What I did do for my year in L.A., the year of 1999, was sin up a storm. I did nothing of consequence. *Who cares what I do, right? I'm damaged goods now. My life has no consequence. I'm free!* I called it my "cremation of care" year—named after the cremation of care ceremony the powerful folks practice at the well-known Bohemian Club. The difference is, they only do cremation of care for a few days out of the year—let go of care about their responsibilities, the world and its problems, and just party with their friends and colleagues. But I did it for my whole year in L.A.!

I drank and went to movies. I rented movies, and drank. I golfed. I played seven-card stud at the Crystal Park Casino in Compton. And I was often out late at night, doing other sinful things. Oh, and did I mention I drank? And I did all this while living off the inheritance from my grandparents that I mentioned at the beginning of this book.

In short, there was nothing "spiritual" about this year at all, at least on the surface of things. I was behaving as a sinner through and through. And why not? I had nothing to lose. I'd already lost myself, after The Plunge, so what the hell? I just didn't care anymore, about anything. At least for a little while.

I should mention that I made a very good friend while I lived in Redondo Beach. She was my neighbor, and on many of my nights out, I was hanging with her. In effect, she was my only close friend and company that year. All my other friends and family were busy with their lives, living in different parts of the state.

Though I was attracted to her, she had an on-again off-again boyfriend, and so while there was some flirting going on, no romance of any kind ever started between us. Really, it was not shocking that she didn't want to date me—I was way out of shape, drank like a fish, smoked like a chimney, and was living an aimless, purposeless life with literally no future prospects.

I bring her up because at the end of my year in L.A., I'd been talking to her on the phone while riding in my friends' car. Thinking I had hung up the phone, I made some very unkind remarks to my friends about her—a dismissive joke of some kind that was really sarcastic and mean. My friend pointed out that the phone had not hung up; we were still connected.

Realizing she might have heard, I felt absolutely terrible. There is no doubt that I was being passive-aggressive and mean because of my subconscious anger that she didn't, in fact, want to date me. Anyway, as it turns out, she must have heard my comment, because she stopped returning my calls after that, and I never saw her again.

Today I can say I am very grateful to have been her friend. She really was a godsend during my time in L.A.—a very isolated time in my life—and I feel a lot of love for her now. I hope someday she will forgive me.

BTW, as I write this, the Dolphins just knocked off the mighty Patriots on their last game of the NFL season, putting a nice little feather in their cap. Just thought I'd mention this, on the one-in-a-million chance she ever reads this.

EIGHTEEN

Arriving at Rock Bottom

As 1999 came to a close, it somehow finally occurred to me that life wasn't working for me in L.A. Without much fanfare or notice, I decided to move back up to northern California, to see if I could do something worthwhile there.

I don't remember if I got the idea to return to USF to finally finish my bachelor's degree while I was still in L.A., or if I did that after returning. Either way, that's what I ended up doing upon my return to northern California in early 2000.

Going back to complete my undergraduate degree (in Business Marketing) was about the only redeemable thing I did in my northern California return, unless I can count working for my brother's friend selling gelato for awhile. I wasn't very good at that, and the job did not last long. What *is* noteworthy, for the sake of this story, is that when I returned to northern California, I moved into a little apartment in Mill Valley with my cousin Caspian and my friend Adrian. Mill Valley, of course, is where this story began.

I spent another year pissing away my life, burning through my inheritance, and drinking a ton (more) in Mill Valley. As I said, I at least managed to finish my bachelor's degree in the process. But more mayhem, more sinning, more golf—and lower and lower my sense of self-worth slid. Besides the degree, I did get a hole-in-one that year(!)—my only other meaningful accomplishment. Yes, I bought drinks for everyone back at the clubhouse.

And so, as the year 2000 approached its close, we have arrived where we began this story. For it is at this time that I would have my epiphany about not having fun, and then, one week later—on that fateful night—bombing with Lynette, the pretty, friendly bartender/server who started off this story. I was miserable; I was going nowhere. And I had officially arrived at rock bottom.

As it turns out, rock bottom is a great place to be, provided you survive it. For often, this is where the real spiritual journey begins. And so it did for me.

NINETEEN

An Intervention

I WAKE UP in the morning, groggy and numb. I don't want to remember the night before, when I had humiliated myself in front of Lynette. So I tuck the whole thing squarely in the back of my mind. I have no idea what I'm going to do today, or in a broader sense, at all.

Then my phone rings and it's my mom, who is inviting me up to her house for a visit in Sonoma. With nothing better to do, I get in my car and make the fifty-minute drive up to Sonoma from Mill Valley in a daze.

I am still reeling from the night before. And I feel... odd, in a slightly different state than the day before. Maybe nothing more than a slight shift; it's nothing I can put my finger on. All I know is, it didn't take long for the Universe to respond after I hit rock bottom, after my *there must be another way* moment.

I arrive at Mom's house and walk into her kitchen, where she stands looking at me with a funny expression. She seems a bit nervous, and it appears there is an agenda to this invitation to visit.

She doesn't waste any time. It's an ambush. She plops

a twelve-step recovery book down on the kitchen counter right in front of me and says, "I think you have a drinking problem and that you need to quit drinking." I'm stunned. I just stand there, in shocked silence. Then she adds, "I am doing this because I am very worried about the plans you have made with Adrian."

Basically, a week or so earlier, in the middle of my "epiphany" week, Adrian had scored a couple of free airline tickets to fly anywhere in the world. Naturally, we chose Bangkok, Thailand. Mom was afraid she'd never see me again. What's amazing is that she had no idea what had happened the night before with Lynette, and that it couldn't have been a more perfect time to invite me up and drop this bomb on me.

I mentioned earlier I don't believe in coincidences, and here is a perfect example of why. Had she tried to get me to quit drinking *any* other day, I'm sure I would have given her the proverbial finger. In fact, an intervention specialist friend of my therapist had already tried an intervention on me, and I had ignored her. But on this particular morning, I was so *down*, so defeated by my life, that my mind and heart really were open for change. After what had happened the night before, what I'll call—for now—a Higher Power apparently knew that, because the very next day, the next morning, my mom decides to hold a one-person intervention!

I knew she was right, and thankfully there were enough sane brain cells left in my head that I heard her, and I canceled my trip to Thailand. Instead, I flipped through a bunch of alcohol and drug rehab brochures that had been sitting on my dresser for at least a month, given to me by the earlier interveners, and I found a brochure for an alcohol and drug treatment facility that looked like the perfect fit for me. It was about as far away from Sonoma/Mill Valley/Bay Area/L.A./California as I could get: Florida. This treatment facility emphasized heavy individual and group therapy, and there was a picture of palm trees and a golf course on the cover. God knows, I knew that after The Plunge, with the constant fear of another plunge lingering always at the back of my mind, combined with all my drinking madness, I needed far more than to just quit drinking. Though I was still in therapy and still on meds, I knew I needed a complete psychological overhaul. So I booked a flight to depart November 4th, 2000, to Fort Lauderdale, Florida, and off I would go. But not before one more night on the town.

It is no small thing to consider giving up drinking, given my upbringing and my relationship to wine and the wine business. You would think it was the most challenging decision I ever had to make. But it wasn't. I was *done*. Later, when I was in twelve-step recovery, I would be quietly, deeply grateful that I didn't struggle at all with sobriety, with relapsing, like many others do in recovery. I was *done*. It was the first, immediate gift of The Plunge. I understood that if I continued to live a loose life, it was not a matter of *if*, but *when* there would be another incident of some kind. The doctors assured it. I was *done*.

My cousin Caspian, one of my best friends Ben,

Adrian and I all went out in Sonoma the night before I was set to leave for Florida and begin rehab the next morning. I was officially saying goodbye to alcohol. We went out to dinner at Piatti—a long-since-closed restaurant—and brought three special bottles of wine along; one supplied by me and two by Ben. I opened a bottle of our 1974 Gundlach Bundschu Zinfandel, one of the earliest wines we produced in the new era, and one that had always been among my favorites. Ben then opened an older vintage Opus One. And the third bottle I've completely forgotten, but it was old and probably valuable, too. We enjoyed the wines with dinner, and even shared some of it with some of the other diners at the restaurant, including my roommate AJ, who was there with some friends. I don't remember tasting the wines at all. I was too nervous about what was to come.

After dinner, we headed over to Steiner's, a long-time local bar on the Sonoma plaza, for a drink or two. Then we moved on over to the Swiss Hotel, another plaza institution. There, I ordered the very last alcoholic drink I have ever had. A Bud Light. That may sound crazy to some. Why not finish with the Zin? Or something else maybe even more special? Why? Because I was a drinker. And I knew it.

Over the years (I was thirty years old that night), I'd had many cocktails and many, many bottles of wine. But my staple, the drink I went to with my friends most often, the drink I/we bought case after case of, was Bud Light. It had to do with calories and trying to stay fit, at least early on, and, well, it's what young twenty-somethings often drink.

So I drank my Bud Light, all the while noticing that I wasn't drunk at all, despite all the wine and maybe a cocktail or two I had had earlier in the evening. I was too much on edge. In fact, I believe it was a somber, awkward night for everyone involved. It was for me. No fireworks or cheers or laughter; rather, there was a sense of sadness. It kinda felt like I was going to prison. But my friends and cousin, whom I love, persevered with me, and together we made my final rounds around Sonoma's long-established watering holes. My life as I knew it was coming to an end. I was leaving for Florida the next morning, and it felt as if I was headed for the end of the world.

Turns out that wasn't far from the truth.

TWENTY

Renaissance

"WHAT's your goal for coming here?" asked one of the intake counselors. I was sitting in a plastic office chair, facing her in her little office. It was my first day at my new home, the Renaissance Institute, an alcohol and drug treatment facility located in Delray Beach, Florida.

I said, "I just want to be happy-go-lucky Robbie and not drink."

She laughed out loud and said, "That's not going to work. And let's not call you Robbie, let's call you Rob."

She had my attention.

How could she have known that way back when I was a freshman at UC Davis (my first university before I transferred to USF), I wanted to change my name from Robbie—my childhood name—to Rob? When I'd arrived at Davis, I had introduced myself as Rob to all my new college friends. It worked great, until about a month later, when my old high school friends came for a visit. After a a beer or two, my new friends overheard my old friends bellowing, "Roooobbbbiie..." late into the night, and my new friends seemed to like that name better. Robbie became the name that stuck. I didn't have enough inner conviction to demand everyone call me Rob; so Robbie it was.

Yet here, at the very beginning of my recovery journey, this counselor hit the nail on the head! I would be a big fan of her, along with the whole Renaissance staff, from that moment forward. [Note: I go by Rob to most people today, but some of my old friends still call me Robbie. I don't have a preference anymore].

Renaissance Institute consisted of a pink apartment building, located adjacent to a golf course, and an office complex a mile or two away where all the individual and group therapy happened. Us patients/residents lived in the apartment complex and followed a strict set of rules. They ran a tight ship there. We had to keep our apartments, including the bathrooms, spotless, lest there be consequences (I don't remember what they were). We cooked our own meals. We had to wake between six and seven most mornings. Then daily, we would be bussed over to the office complex for therapy. I had two roommates, one a recovering heroin addict, and I can't remember the other's affliction—coke, I think. What struck me most about both of them was that they seemed like normal guys. At that time, I didn't know heroin had reached the mainstream. Anyway, overall, it was a bit like boot camp, in that it was very strict, regimented and orderly. I adjusted okay to everything.

What amazed me was that about a day or two after

I had arrived (and began to sober up), I was in our little apartment in the morning, watching an ad for a sitcom on TV. One of the characters made a joke, and I actually laughed! I felt a real laugh in my belly, and I was quite startled. It was as if I was laughing for the first time, and it felt good. I think it was a sign that I was on the right track, given that I was pretty dazed and confused at this point.

My stay at Renaissance lasted for about four months, and though a lot of healing and recovering, as well as significant drama, happened during that time, I don't care to share too much about it. In general, as I began to heal and learn a bunch of psychological stuff about myself, my drinking, and my life and relationships, I definitely began to get better. I learned about alcoholism, addiction, dysfunctional family roles like the hero and the scapegoat (I'm the scapegoat), and other concepts that helped me to get a grasp on things. And I stayed sober through it all. On this point, again, I was one of the lucky ones. Overall, this was an important point on my journey and I am grateful for it.

Besides therapy, which included some "tough love" involving counselors screaming at us for poor behavior in residence, Renaissance also introduced us all to twelve-step recovery. Along with the counseling, especially my individual therapy, this introduction to the twelve steps was a big step on my own spiritual journey.

In short, I was still not a "spiritual" person at this time (even though I'd been to hell). A couple of years prior, after I had started to recover from hell (The Plunge) and

The Plunge 2.0, I had put down the angel book (and any-thing like it) and had sunk back into the world—see me in 1999 in L.A. for reference. So there was nothing spiritual happening when I arrived at Renaissance. Note: I would later learn there is *always* something spiritual happening, but I sure was not aware of it at that time.

What I did have going for me was that my mind re-mained fairly open. As alluded to above, The Plunge and its aftermath had, unbeknownst to me, taken a BIG bite out of my ego. My mind was really open for anything, at least to a degree. Looking back, during my time at Re-naissance, I was in a sort-of "teach me/guide me, *I will fol-low"* state of mind. Thus, I was mentally prepared—with-out any conscious planning on my own—for just about anything that came my way.

And what came my way was twelve-step recovery, along with its heavy emphasis on this "God" business.

TWENTY-ONE

Florida

"Let's face it, some people simply do not belong..." said Judge Smails to Ty Webb in one of my all-time favorite movies, *Caddyshack*. The Judge, played by late actor Ted Knight, was pretty much summing up how I felt about myself in relation to Alcoholics Anonymous, or AA, the Twelve Step recovery program I had chosen to join. When Renaissance introduced me to it, I was willing and able to join, because as I mentioned, I was willing to do about anything around then. But over time, I learned that I was willing only to go so far with AA.

After "graduating" from Renaissance, I made the epic decision to stay in Florida for awhile, rather than returning to California. I felt I needed more time to recover, and I didn't want to leave the good work we'd started in therapy.

On a typical day for me during this time in Florida, I would wake up, go to work at a job I had gotten, or I'd go to a bookstore if I wasn't working. Then I'd go to therapy in the afternoon, and then go to an AA meeting in the evening. When I'd get to the meeting, I would walk in, sit in the back, and listen to everyone else share about their "experience, strength, and hope." I rarely spoke (or "shared") myself, a little bit because I was still deathly afraid of public speaking, but also—mostly—because I was very, very angry.

I had learned early in therapy that my personality, a beta personality, featured a heavy dose of people pleasing. In other words, for most of my young life, I had done what others wanted me to do, or what I believed others wanted me to do, at the expense of doing what, in my heart, I myself wanted to do.

For instance, did I really want to spend all day in the hot summer sun picking up rocks out in a barren field like my dad asked me to? I don't think so, but the thing is, at the time I didn't know there was an option. I just did it. It was the same with my friends, or teachers, or any sort of authority figure. I did what they wanted me to do most of the time. And I was wholly unaware of the unconscious resentment and anger that built up over the years from doing the will of others.

I should add that I could be stubborn. Occasionally, if I felt really strongly about something, only then would I be willing to say "no" to someone. But this was rare. Most of the time, I was a doormat.

It was in early therapy that I learned of this doormat quality in my personality. So I decided early on, in relation to everything, including AA, that, "I am doing everything *my* way now." So that characterized my time in AA.

Many suggestions are made in AA to help newcomers to stay sober. I followed some, like attending 90 meetings in 90 days, but completely ignored others, including the main one. In AA, they guide you to get a sponsor (an AA mentor) and work the Twelve Steps as soon as you are ready and willing. I said "hell no" to that, and did it my way. My way was to show up, listen, and leave. I didn't want to "join" the community. Didn't want to make any new friends (though I did eventually make a couple of friends while I was there, including my good friend Michelle). I didn't want to do anything, really. And why should I? I stayed sober, and I *was* growing and learning.

Along with attending AA meetings, I was going to therapy regularly. Though I don't wish to share too much about this, I will say that therapy was a big part of my life in Florida. I developed a professional, yet close, personal relationship with my therapist, and so for several years I needed no friends at all but my relationship with her. I happily lived a life of relative isolation, going to bookstores, going to the beach, going to the movies and out to eat, going to therapy, and going to meetings, while I did all this flying solo. I loved my life in these first years of sobriety, and learned a lot about myself. It was also at this time that I began to learn about spirituality.

TWENTY-TWO

A Step in the Right Direction

STEP 3. *(We) Made a decision to turn our will and our lives over to the care of God as we understood Him.*

THIS IS the third step of the twelve steps of Alcoholics Anonymous. As you can see, "God" is central to the step. In fact, He is central in several other steps, and really, is the center of the whole program. The writers added *"as we understood Him"* so people new to the program wouldn't go running for the hills. The founders understood that a lot of drunks wanted nothing to do with "God," so they added this clause. Newcomers working the steps could decide just about anything or anyone could be God for them, as long as they were willing to perceive their God as a "power greater than themselves." Long story short, it has worked for many people for many years, and it worked for me.

Though I didn't follow all the suggestions in AA, it is noteworthy that I didn't have a severe reaction to the "God" business when I arrived in AA. That was one of the great gifts of The Plunge. I'd experienced an alternate reality, a Devil figure, so maybe there was a God, too. I was open to it. So while all the "God" business can and has turned off many an AA'er, I was okay with it. Yet at the same time, I didn't dive right in and become a born-again *Big Book* (AA Book) Thumper, either. As I said earlier, I just kept an open mind, and kept on going to meetings. No special prayers or practices beyond that.

Overall, through my years in AA, I think all the talk of God, community and sharing in those meetings melted any of my lingering resistance to the idea of God. In fact, my mind *must* have continued to open to the idea of God, because of what happened after just three years or so of not drinking and working on my mind in meetings and in therapy.

TWENTY-THREE

An Affair to Remember

B ETWEEN 2001 and 2003, I was trucking along in Fort Lauderdale, living, working, going to meetings. And, oh yeah, I was having an affair. Is that what you call it when the woman is the one cheating on her boyfriend (and eventual husband), and I am the male version of the mistress—the mister? I don't know. But that is what was happening. How did a person of such high moral character, one as pure as the driven white snow, such as myself, get involved in such a tawdry situation as this? And why? I'll try to explain.

It seemed to happen by chance. I guess they all do. In 2001, I decided to go to the Art Institute of Fort Lauderdale, initially to pursue a degree in photography. I was looking for a new career. And I was also very single, available, and on the market at the time. There happened to be a couple of attractive young women in one of my classes. I noticed them but never talked to them, and I generally kept my distance. I sat on the opposite side of the room and did my best to pretend *not* to notice them. I suppose I'd been doing this since grade school.

The room was made up of tables seating four people each. One day, I walked into class, and, rather than slinking over to my corner as usual, I somehow got up the nerve to sit at a table where one of the young women was sitting. Then, to my surprise, the *other* young woman walked into class and sat down next to me! So now I was at the same table as both of these attractive women. I tried as best I could to pay attention to the professor that day, but I probably failed miserably.

Well, I must have said or done something right, because a few weeks later I found myself having coffee with the young woman who had come into class and sat next to me. In order to protect the innocent and the lovely, I will not say her name, but we slowly began to develop a relationship. I would learn that she was from a foreign country, had a boyfriend, and I would learn after a couple of years of "dating" her (if that's what you want to call it), that she had secretly married her boyfriend, who was American. When I eventually confronted her about this, she said she did this "in order to stay in the country." It was a Green Card issue, but I believe she loved him, too.

She and I saw each other on and off for about four years, and we did communicate that we had feelings for each other. We loved each other, in a way. Yet there was also a lot of conflict between us, because I ultimately wanted her to end her relationship with her boyfriend/ husband. Promises were made, complex issues emerged, lots of drama ensued, but her breakup with him never manifested. And so it ended up not working out.

The theme of this book is the spiritual journey, and so I try to associate everything that has happened in my life in these terms. So what was the purpose of my affair with this lovely woman, whom I will always appreciate and have fond feelings for? Well, in my opinion, some of it was for me to learn personal relationship issues and dynamics. These kind of things you can discuss in a therapy session. I learned more about myself after having spent time with her. But on another level, I firmly believe I had this affair for a bigger reason.

Let's face it—given the philandering proclivities I alluded to earlier, during my drinking days, and now this affair with her, it became clear that I was not the most saintly of persons. In fact, there was a serious dark side to my personality, and in many instances and in many ways, I was not a kind man.

My new therapist, who happened to be female, said to me not long after I had arrived in Florida, "You are ambivalent towards women, aren't you?"

At the time, I didn't really understand what she was saying. But now I do, and I admit that I was. I had a love/hate relationship toward women. In my mind, I had denied the "hate" part of it, believing I only loved women. But it was clear from my *actions* that there was an element of hate in me. I don't want to get into the weeds of psychology, but I would learn that this ambivalence stretched far beyond just my feelings for women. *A Course in Miracles* would teach me much more, as I will relate later.

I would like to put this all into religious terms, too,

since religion and God were now something I was beginning to learn about as I began life in sobriety. To put it simply, in religious terms—especially after the affair: I am a sinner. BIG TIME. A big-time sinner. According to millions of Christians, not to mention believers from other religions, I am a sinner through and through, and bound for eternal hell. I have not accepted Jesus into my life (in the way traditional Christians require), and so my soul is doomed. (It still amazes me that millions of Christians would tell me this is a fact, right now, if I asked them). The point I'm trying to make is that I am *far* from a saint, at least from most people's perception, and many would say I do not even deserve to go to Heaven, "to be saved."

TWENTY-FOUR

A Completely Unexpected Invitation

I AM SITTING on my couch on a Sunday morning sometime in 2003, flipping through the channels on my twenty-four-inch flat-screen TV. My little nine hundred-square-foot house is located in the city of Wilton Manors, a suburb of Fort Lauderdale. Though there are cars whizzing by on the busy street just past my front lawn outside my living room, the noise goes unnoticed, because I've lived here for a while and have grown accustomed to it. Bullwinkle, one of my two cats, a charcoal grey bruiser, jumps up on my lap, purring and looking for a scratch. His sister Nonie is off hunting spiders somewhere around the house.

I haven't seen *her* (my affair) in months because we are in the middle of one of our "off-times." It is a lazy Sunday morning, so why not watch a little TV? Life is good.

Flipping around, I find a station with a young preacher giving the good news to an arena full of people. After The Plunge, and continuing into my time in AA, I am now unmistakably spiritually curious, so I have no problem staying on this station and listening in for a while.

My, how times have changed. Just a few short years ago, I would have projected a vicious and cruel thought or two at the preacher, and maybe even Jesus himself, and then changed the channel. But not now.

The preacher's name is Joel Osteen. I listen to him for a short time, and by then I am completely drawn in. He is sharing a lovely message of positivity and hope, and everyone in his audience is captivated, including me. I love his stories and his Southern drawl, and I must say I find his voice soothing and relaxing.

That's why at the end of his sermon, I don't have any problem when he signs off his sermon with, "'Lord Jesus, I repent of my sins. Come into my heart. Wash me clean. I'll make you my Lord. Friend, if you prayed that simple prayer, we believe you got born again." Amazingly, this very religious language doesn't seem to turn me off at all.

Without consciously trying to, I found myself watching Joel almost every weekend for awhile. Finally at some point, on one of those Sunday mornings, at the end of his sermon, I said, "What the hell? Couldn't hurt." So I closed my eyes and repeated the above prayer about making Jesus my Lord. I actually did it! And I *meant* my prayer, too. Effectively speaking, I said, "I'll make you my Lord Jesus, but I don't have *any idea* what that means or what will happen, but I mean it. I am inviting You into my heart." I really did mean it, too.

Did I go join a church after that? No. Did I join Joel's church? No. Did I start reading the Bible? No. Did I become a born-again and go around trying to convert everyone? No. Did I vow to permanently end my sinful relationship with *her*? Hell no. But I must say, I did want to invite Jesus into my heart. I just had an intuitive feeling this would be a good thing. And so, that's what I did.

There are a couple of reasons I wanted to share this story. First, because my time with Joel and my introduction to Jesus is a big part of my journey. The second is that I believe this story is directly related to events that were to follow.

At this time, I have to confess that I had become a fairly prayerful guy. Besides praying with Joel every Sunday morning, I was in the habit of getting on my knees every day and praying a prayer of thanks for all my blessings. This habit of prayer I picked up in AA, and it would last for a couple of years.

My prayer was very simple. It went something like this, "Dear God, thank You for the roof over my head, the food in my belly, and the clothes on my back." And that was it. From there, I might add other thoughts, like, "Let me do Your Will and not mine," and "Let me be of service." Often I'd add in my prayers, "I don't know what any of this means or even if You can hear or even if there is any effect, but I'll keep praying." And so, prayer to God and Jesus, among other things, is what I was up to there in my little house just outside Fort Lauderdale. I never told anyone about this. Just kept it between me and God and Jesus, if they were around.

Who knew if any of this would have any effect? I mean, I've already said it — I'm a big-time sinner. Who

would listen to my prayers?
    And yet…

TWENTY-FIVE

Up To Heaven

The Great Light always surrounds you
and shines out from you.
—ACIM T-11.III.4:7

Iᴛ's sᴏᴍᴇᴛɪᴍᴇ in 2003, around 11:45 p.m., and I'm at home, sitting on the couch, watching TV (again). It's a typical night, which means I'm watching the Jay Leno opening monologue before I go to bed. I do this most nights, because I love his light-hearted sense of humor. So this night is like every other. I turn the TV off and head to bed, with the kitties following along. Everything is normal, as far as I know.

Oddly, I have no journal entry of this night, even though it would end up being the most significant night of my life. I had been keeping a detailed journal at this time, and I would one day go through all my journals, trying to find an entry for this day, but I never could. Anyway, as I said, nothing special seemed to be happening. Just going to bed on another given night.

Then I fell asleep and had a dream like no dream I've ever had before or since:

I'm sitting in a large sports stadium, not unlike where the San Francisco Giants play, and it's nighttime. The stadium is lit by the tall towering lights. I look around and see that all the seats are empty besides mine. I am completely alone in the stadium—or so I think. I am sitting way up high, in the nosebleed seats towards the top of the stadium, in right field, looking straight down onto the field below. It appears as if they are setting up for some sort of show or concert, but I can't be sure of what.

Then, for no particular reason, I feel prompted to turn around and look back up behind me, towards the top of the stadium. That's when I see a figure walking down the steep stadium steps above me, descending towards me, just a couple of seats to my left. The figure is dark and I can't make out his features, other than that he is of average height, wearing contemporary clothes, and I can barely make out sandy blond hair. Otherwise, I cannot see his face or any other features because there is a warm, bright light shining all around his body, putting him in silhouette.

Instantly, I recognize that it is Jesus who is walking down the steps! Both startled and deeply elated, I cannot overstate how happy I am to see him. I have never felt happier in my life, either waking or dreaming, than I feel at this moment. Really, I am just beside myself, like a kid on Christmas morning facing a mountain of presents. Or like a long-lost and lonely child who is suddenly reunited with his brother. Nowhere in my mind are the angry and hateful feelings I once had for him. It is as if they never existed. I simply cannot contain my joy. It's Jesus!! Who knew I loved the guy so much?

Then after a moment, I notice that there is someone else following him down the stairs. It is my old best friend, Jon. In a flash, my joy disappears, and in its place I feel a biting jealousy. "Hey. Why does *he* get to hang out with Jesus and not me!?" Though I still consider him a great friend, Jon and I always were quite competitive. Anyway, my anger then vanishes just as quickly, as I answer my own question: "Who cares? It's Jesus!" I'm just so happy to be there with him, nothing else matters.

As he descends the stairs and approaches my row of seats, I become worried that he will not notice me or acknowledge me. But my fears are quickly put to rest, because when he arrives at my row, Jesus stops and slowly begins to turn to his right, towards me. No thoughts or words are exchanged between us, but as I watch, the warm bright light that was surrounding his body now seems to get even brighter. As he turns towards me, so does the light, until by the time Jesus' body is facing me, I cannot even see him, or Jon, or the stadium, or anything at all. The shining light has completely blotted out all forms, and now I am completely enveloped in light. There is nothing but a soft, neutral whiteness everywhere, and I am not frightened at all, but I am, for a moment, a little startled …

… *Then I am lifted into Heaven.*

It is truly an unspeakable experience, but I will try to explain.

The soft, neutral whiteness instantly disappears, and I find myself *lifted* out of the quiet but happy dream, and into an ecstatic, blissful, all-encompassing Light. I wish to gently but *strongly* emphasize here that I am no longer dreaming. I am in Heaven. It is a state of such a high vibration and purity that there are literally no words or experiences on Earth that can compare. An extraordinary, unspeakable love and bliss is suddenly all I know, and the experience is so intense that it is nearly overwhelming. *Everything is Light.*

When Jesus said, "I am the light of the world," it turns out he meant it literally. And he also meant that he was not alone as the Light of the world. *We all are.*

Instantly, I am crying a stream of tears of ecstatic joy, and I reach up instinctively to wipe them away, only to learn that there are no tears or face for them to stream down. They are more like ideas in my mind. Quickly the sense of tears, face and body are gone, and I am pure being in this Light. I am in a state of what I can only describe as pure abstraction. There are no specifics or forms of any kind like there is in our world.

Simultaneously, I am aware that I am anything but alone. I am in fact in the presence of God Himself —and I am in a state of complete *Awe.* And He is communicating nothing but a deep, abundant, all-encompassing Love— for me! I am literally shining in Joy. It is an experience of what I would later learn is called oneness, or our natural state, or our true home. It is the experience of revelation.

While in a state of abstract being, shining in the Light,

God communicated with me directly—without words or specific thoughts—the message I believe I am meant to share. As I understand it, it is a message everyone will learn eventually, but only when they *wish* to learn it. I believe that for now, to many readers, it will only be an intellectual idea and will have relatively little meaning. In order to really understand the message, a person must *wish* to learn the truth first, then be led on a journey, and ultimately learn the message for themselves. That is why the theme of this book is the spiritual journey. It has been so helpful for me and my peace of mind that I wanted to share it with others, in case they are ready to make that wish for themselves.

The message communicated to me by God was simply regarding my state of eternal Innocence. I cannot describe the feeling of elation I feel when He gently shares with me my Innocence. And I come to understand that this message of Innocence extends way beyond any specific moment from my life, or anyone else's, for that matter. Our Innocence is absolute and universal. His communication is the fact of my Divine Innocence, no matter what horrible sinful thought, word, or deed I have ever committed back on Earth in this life or any other. All of that is literally *nothing* to Him. Only my Innocence is real. I cannot describe how blissfully joyful I am when He shares my Innocence with me. It is indescribable.

And what I like to call our Original Innocence, clearly, does not belong to me alone. He was sharing that *all humanity* is Divinely Innocent. In the end, all of our so called sins—no matter how egregious they seem to be—have no effect on God's judgement of us. He loves us forever and forever. This was the message that was given me. And so that is what I am sharing here with you.

The other thing I experienced while I was there, is that I was not there alone with God. Rather, on a very deep intuitive level, I understood that we are *all* there. I understood *no one* is left out. Heaven is not an exclusive resort for the religiously special. It is One Big Party for us all!

In the end, we will all return there.

I can't really say more at this point. I believe with total certainty that everyone will have an experience of Revelation sooner or later. It may be next week, or in the next lifetime (for those who choose to believe in reincarnation). But it will happen. All I can say is that it was apparently my time in this life.

I spent a lot of time asking, "Why me?" I had *no* clue this was going to happen that night in 2003 when I went to bed. It seems that God's Spirit, the Holy Spirit, Who lives in us, *knows* us a lot better than we know ourselves. I'll leave it at that.

I am hesitant to describe Heaven beyond this brief re-telling. I do not wish to attempt a description of the indescribable any more than I already have. I would, though, like to share Jesus' description of revelation, which he shares in *A Course in Miracles*:

> *Revelation is intensely personal and cannot be meaningfully translated. That is why any attempt to describe it in*

words is impossible. Revelation induces only experience ...
Revelation is literally unspeakable because it is an experi-
ence of unspeakable love.

Awe should be reserved for revelation, to which it is
perfectly and correctly applicable... — ACIM T-1.II.2:1-7

This is my holy little secret. The thing I never talk
about with anyone, but is always on my mind. This story
is the central event on my spiritual journey. I'm sharing
this experience because I feel prompted to do so, and also
because I hope it may be helpful and comforting to someone, somewhere. Because God—there is God, as it turns
out—chose to lift *me,* an ordinary drunk, a big-time "sinner" with some serious psych issues, *up to Heaven.*

TWENTY-SIX

Back on Earth

I WOKE UP suddenly the next morning, back in my bed in Wilton Manors, back on Earth. I sat up with a little smile on my face, with a very light sense of peace and joy swirling around me. Everything looked normal: the small room, the bed, the little bathroom off to my right. But the peace of Heaven did not completely evaporate until after a couple of minutes. As far as I can remember, *Wow* was my only thought. Though I didn't necessarily understand what had just happened, and had no context to put it into, it did feel comfortable, and even natural. There was a sense of "no big deal," even though I intuitively understood there was literally no *bigger* deal in my life.

The next time I met with my therapist, I told her all about it. At the end of my long, passionate retelling, she seemed to take it all in stride.

Then she said (and I'm paraphrasing here), "That sounds great, Rob, but let's keep you down here on Earth. You still haven't found your career or vocation yet. And maybe you'd like to meet someone else, who's not involved in a relationship already ..."

She was referring to my affair, of course, along with my decidedly incomplete life. Looking back, it was the perfect advice at the time. Keep in mind that she had heard all the rest: the excessive drinking, all the gory details of The Plunge, the hospitalizations, etc. She understood better than I that my psyche was sensitive and pretty battered from my crazy life.

So the best course was to live simply, on the ground, on Earth. I must have agreed with her, because I followed her guidance, as I usually did. Though I never forgot about it, obviously, I put the Revelation behind me almost immediately and went back to living my normal life for the next several years.

I think it should be noted, though, that I didn't suddenly become enlightened after the Revelation. Not even close. My ego was definitely alive and well. I would continue to have the same struggles and self-doubts as before. You could say that there was still a cork in miracles for me. A miracle, as *A Course in Miracles* teaches, is simply a correction, a *shift in perception* in the mind, from fear to love, from blame to forgiveness, which results in an expression of love. We do it all the time—perform miracles (or express love), though most of us don't think of it that way.

But so often, we don't heed the correction. We don't make the shift in our mind, and so our expressions of love are "corked," or bottled up, or blocked by our identification with the ego—which always causes perceptions of fear and guilt, resulting in feelings and expressions of fear and guilt. Thus, though it obviously helped me on the journey, the Revelation didn't pop the cork all the way out of the miracle bottle. I continued to spend virtually all my time identifying with the ego—a concept I knew little about. But I'd say it did help loosen the cork a little!

There is no doubt that nothing would be quite the same after the Revelation either. I was given a glimpse of where we will all end. Or rather, where we all are now, but are not aware of it. It was cool. And a very big deal. But experiencing Revelation was definitely not the end of the road for me. And according to *A Course in Miracles*, it's not for most people who have experienced it. In a sense, it is just the beginning.

We're given a glimpse of our true home, and then we've got to come back here and do the work, in order to begin uncorking miracles all the way out of the miracle bottle, and get back there permanently.

How do I get from where I am now, as a flawed, guilt-ridden human, back to that? This became the quiet, unspoken question in my mind. But, again, I didn't do anything special after the Revelation, at least at first. I just kept going to work, meetings, therapy, beach, and her (for a little longer). And that was it for the next two or three years.

TWENTY-SEVEN

A Transformation of a Sort

T HEN one day, for no particular reason, in my sixth year of sobriety (2006), three years after the Revelation, I just decided to do those damn steps at last. I saw a guy speak at an AA meeting and liked what he said. I asked him to be my sponsor. And together, over the next few months, meeting every week at a Starbucks in downtown Fort Lauderdale, we worked the steps.

The result was unexpected, and totally awesome. It is apparently relatively common for people to go through a transformation of a sort after working the twelve steps, and that's what happened for me. Instead of running through the specifics of what happened while working the steps, most of which I can't remember anyway, let me share what I wrote about *after* finishing, when I met up with my family on a holiday in Mexico:

I'm sitting at the table with my family playing cards, and I simply can't believe what I am seeing and experiencing. There, across the table from me, is my dad. Nancy is to my left, along with my sister-in-law Liz, and Katie. And to my right is Jeff, my ever-tormenting but always-protective older brother, with his two daughters, my nieces Eva and Gracie. It's 2006, and we have all come together for the first time in a long time, on a Thanksgiving holiday in Mexico, at a secluded beach house about an hour north of Puerto Vallarta. I can't really grasp what I'm witnessing, though I would learn years later that what I am experiencing is a miracle, at least according to *A Course in Miracles*.

What I am feeling as I sit and talk and laugh with my family is a simple, quiet peace, a shift of mind. I'm just happy to be here, quiet, and present. I'm truly present with my family for the first time in my life. We are all just sitting around playing cards, and I am having a ball. I would learn some time after this that the rest of the family wasn't having quite as much fun. There were problems with the house, the food, and a host of other things. But I was hardly aware of it. I was having too good of a time.

I cannot fully express what this simple, seemingly common experience meant to me. I was in a state of disbelief, almost shock. For the first time in my thirty-six years of life, I was able to be with my family wholly, without any hidden, unconscious feelings of guilt or resentment. (Or, if there were any, they had been substantially reduced).

Instead, I was able to just easily laugh joyfully with them. It was as if a heavy, dense, invisible shield in my mind that had stood permanently between my family (and really everyone) and myself had been lifted. A heavy weight had been removed, and a feeling of lightness and ease and peace was there to replace it. I felt like a part of my family, truly, for the very first time. And I could not contain my joy at this experience. To me, it was nothing less than a miracle.

For the past few years, I'd gone to meetings and appeared to get a little better as time passed. But I retained a lot of anger and resentment towards my family and certain friends from my past, and really, at a deeper level, towards the whole world and myself. I continued to live in the victim mentality of, "Look what you've done to me!" I would learn, years later, this is certainly not the way to happiness.

Then I met with my new sponsor, who was kind, funny, quirky and very smart, and he proceeded to help me work through the steps. Ultimately, working those twelve steps helped me see that it was not my family or friends or past or the world that was the problem. They helped me see that *I* — my thoughts, beliefs, and attitude—was the problem. By looking within, I had seen that I was no less guilty of contributing to the conflicts in my life than anyone else, and so I experienced the beginning of forgiveness. Thanks to the work my sponsor and I did, eventually completing the steps, much of my anger and resentment had been lifted.

But I was not really aware of any of this until I joined my family on this trip to Mexico. The trip was planned, not by accident, in my belief, soon after I completed the steps. It seemed as if the universe had arranged a way to see the results of the work I'd done. It was there, when we were all together, sitting around the table, playing cards, that I recognized clearly that a healing had occurred. This change of mind was the miracle, and my very happy Thanksgiving its result.

On one evening towards the end of that week in Mexico, after everyone had gone to bed, I felt the urge to go meditate on a little vista that looked out over the Pacific Ocean. By then I was in a very peaceful state, full of gratitude for what I had experienced with my family earlier in the week. I wanted to join with God and thank Him for the gifts I had been given.

So I sat down and began to meditate. I was not accomplished at meditation and didn't practice much, but I had started on and off before. This mediation was particularly peaceful, and my mind was unusually quiet and content. I was just happy to be, and felt like I was smiling on the inside. After a time, I went pretty deep into silence, and at one point I felt prompted to open my eyes.

That's when I saw it: a little bright, white light was gently floating around in front of me, perhaps a few yards away. It was too bright to be a firefly or any sort of bug. I felt peaceful in its presence, and somehow knew it was a little spark of the Divine, a little symbol of the week of forgiveness I had experienced with my family. I had experienced light before, during the Revelation, so it did not startle me. After a minute or two, it disappeared, and I was happy.

TWENTY-EIGHT

The Devil You Say

I'VE ALWAYS been a beach bum, and one of my favorite things to do was to go to the beach. Maybe it had something to do with my first memory as a child. I love the sand, the air, the sound of the waves, the warm sun on my skin. And I love the activity—or lack thereof. Doing nothing is one of my favorite things to do. At the beach, you can just hang, people watch, maybe read for a little bit. Listen to music, take a nap. Also, I must confess, lying at the beach also gives me a tan, which I always thought made me look better. So it was on one of those outings at the beach, in what turned out to be this fateful year of 2006, that the following happened.

I'm lying on my towel on the sand at the main public beach in Fort Lauderdale, soaking in the sun. It's the afternoon, and it is particularly hot and muggy today. I'm not very comfortable at all. I notice a little puddle of sweat filling up my belly button, and droplets of sweat are dribbling down my sides and face. There are people around, but I'm lying on my back with my eyes closed, not paying much attention. Oh, the things we put ourselves through to get a tan!

Despite the physical discomfort, I am in a peaceful state of mind. In effect, I am half-meditating while lying there on the sand. My mind is calm, and wandering idly from one thought to the next. Then, out of nowhere, the memory of The Plunge comes up again. Very peacefully, now that so much time had passed, I gently replay the entire scene of The Plunge again in my mind. I see the darkness, those sinister eyes, that malevolent creature, the separation experience, everything. I gently review it in my mind's eye. No PTSD. No fear. In truth, I've played this scene over and over again in my mind a thousand times since it happened. It's hard not to. But on this day, peacefully meditating on the beach, reviewing it all once again, a sudden insight, or acknowledgment, comes to me.

For what seems like the very first time in my life, I turn to my own inner authority, rather than deferring to some authority figure outside of me. In this case, I turn to my own inner wisdom, rather than to the therapist I worked with in Sonoma just days after The Plunge. What comes to me in my deep, quiet meditative state, is that The Plunge was not a hallucination, as my therapist assured me it was. No. Lying here in the hot sun, I decide that I did in fact visit hell, and that it was in fact Satan, or the Devil, that I encountered.

This new thought felt right to me, down into the deepest marrow of my bones. It just felt true. What did the therapist know, after all? He wasn't there. I was. Only I knew how awful that experience was. In a way, The

Plunge was like the Revelation, in that it was also indescribable.

What's so significant about this moment for me personally, is that whether I was right or not about hell and the Devil, I had now chosen to turn to my own inner strength, or wisdom, rather than always acquiescing to an authority figure outside of me. And so on this day, I promise myself that no matter what anyone else says, including my therapist, I will hold to this new version or interpretation of The Plunge—that it was *not* an hallucination, but was, in fact, real. The truth.

I think it was at this moment, with this small but admittedly unpleasant epiphany on the beach in the summer of 2006, that my spiritual journey really kicked into high gear. Why? Because Holy Spirit—meaning my right-minded Higher Self—would very soon begin to work overtime to help me eradicate this new belief that the journey to hell had been real. In the end it would be clear that the episode *was* merely a *belief* coming from my mind. I would be shown that the entire event was only a *dream* of going to hell.

So I had come full circle. First deferring to a therapist who had some experience, then rejecting the therapist in favor of my own "authority" (ego), only to discover that the *real* authority was, in fact, my true, Higher Self.

The ego likes to live in the dream, so it would have liked The Plunge to be real. But the self, our true Self, wants us to wake up from the dream. So my Higher Self, my right mind, helped me to wake up and see The Plunge for what it was—a dream. When I could see The Plunge as an hallucination, and be more objective about it, I could now give authority to my true, Higher, right-minded Self. All of this I would learn a little later on, when I found the Course. Since we're talking about beliefs, let me address another one I'd been grappling with since 2003. "Why me?" Why did I get to experience the Revelation? I've already mentioned that I'd been praying a lot around that time, but so what? A lot of people pray, but they don't get whisked off to Heaven through Jesus. Over the years since then, one answer kept coming up, and it is this answer I have stuck with. The simplest answer is the best. I believe He gave me that experience to reassure me that the Light is reality, and Nothing, or nothingness, is illusion—an understanding He knows would help *me* know that everything was going to be okay. That I am safe. That we all are, in the end, safe.

To me it's interesting that the Revelation came almost as a precursor to my working with *A Course in Miracles.* This almost seems the reverse of the natural order of things, but I will not question it for a moment.

I will talk more about the Course below. As I said, it seems the universe needed me to learn the fact that The Plunge was indeed an hallucination, or a dream. And so it was at this time that I would stumble into this "spirituality" business. Or rather, into the Spirituality Section.

TWENTY-NINE

Eckhart Tolle Blows My Mind

OR A little over a year, between 2005 and 2006, I had been working at the Fort Lauderdale Whole Foods Market in the bakery department. It was a good job as jobs go, but after some time, I started to get a little antsy. I wanted to find something else.

I began to put out resumés at several businesses about town, including Barnes & Noble Booksellers, which happened to be across the street from Whole Foods. The reason a job there attracted me is that I love books. Plain and simple. The idea of working with and around books sounded really good to me. So I dropped off my resume at the big island-desk in that huge two-story edifice of the written word, and lo and behold, a week or two later I got a call from their hiring manager. I went in for an interview and got the job.

I believe that there are two kinds of people in the world. There are those who are certain that there is a sort of Divine Order gently guiding them through their life, and those who are certain that they are on their own. For all of my life, I was the latter. But it wasn't too long after

I got the job at Barnes & Noble, and started working with all those wonderful books, that I would stop to think every once in a while, *Hey, wait a minute. Something fishy is going on here* ...
I settled in working at the big store pretty quickly. The people I worked with were all great. And I learned that I wasn't the only book nerd who worked at the store because he loved books. It seems it's a thing. I have to give a shout-out to Alan, my coworker and pal. We spent many an hour hunting down misplaced titles and picking up dirty discarded plastic Starbucks Frappuccino cups.

I loved working for my manager, Renette. And I thoroughly enjoyed being amongst all those books. I spent practically as much time looking at them as I did working with them. Before long, my love of books and my dependability at work proved to be valuable assets, and I got promoted to a lead.

A lead is essentially the manager of a specific section or sections of the bookstore. There was a lead for the children's section, a lead for fiction, one for cooking and home improvement, and so on. So what section of the store did fate put me in charge of? A large section upstairs, including business, languages, computer science, self-improvement, sex and relationships (where I may have slacked off flipping through books a bit more than in other sections), and ...(drumroll please): religion and spirituality.

My job included many responsibilities. One was to keep all the sections up to date, restocking depleted titles, and removing outdated titles. Another was customer assistance, helping folks find the titles they were looking for. For quite some time, I just plodded along, doing my job, occasionally flipping through a book if it captured my interest, like a "how-to-start-a-business book," for instance.

As with all the different sections I worked in, I spent quite some time in the religion and spirituality section. As far as I can remember, I would pause occasionally as I worked to read the back cover of a certain book, or perhaps a paragraph or two of an introduction. I had a very unfocused curiosity for all these spiritual books, and never really felt prompted to dive into any of them in particular (despite having had experienced the Revelation a few short years prior).

However, for several years, I had dreamed of starting my own small business. So I spent countless hours in this store, as well as other bookstores, as a customer, reading business books and start-up magazines—and drinking gallons and gallons of coffee in the process. I thought becoming a businessman, like nearly every other male in my family, was the way for me.

So I wasn't immediately drawn to the spiritual titles. Of course, I was not aware of the great *resistance* I, as well as much of humanity, has to spiritual teachings (Yes, I know there are millions of folks in the metaphysical community today. But there are tens of millions who are not, and it is they of whom I speak). We all love our business and politics and religion and sports and world events, and namely, the world itself. Me included. Who needs spirituality? Anyway, despite the crazy life I'd had, curiously I did not dive right into spirituality, even though I was literally neck-deep in books written by its teachers and authors nearly every day. Then one day, I walked into work and noticed that we had put up an end stack of a new title in this very same religion and spirituality section. The title of the book was called *The Power of Now* by Eckhart Tolle. I paid it scant attention at first, until after one of my shifts a week or two later.

One thing I did that some of my coworkers thought was crazy was that as soon as one of my shifts would end, I would simply transform into a customer and hang around the store. This was unlike my coworkers, who couldn't wait to bolt after their shifts. I'd buy a cup of coffee and start looking around at books and/or magazines. I took a little ribbing for this but didn't mind. I believe it was on one of these post-shift store outings that I was hovering in the spirituality section, and my curiosity finally got the better of me. I picked up this odd title—*How could "now" be powerful?*—and sat down in a big comfy chair with my coffee and began to read the book.

Well, I just ended up binge-reading the whole book. I don't remember if I bought it at first, or just read it in the store. But by the end of my reading, I was truly blown away.

The main point Tolle was making was that if one looks closely, there are no problems—guilt, shame, fear, stress, or any issues at all—in the present moment, right "now." Right *now*, all is well. It is only when our own mind and its thoughts venture into the past or the future (which it does constantly), where regret and worry live side by side, that we experience all our troubles. So the point is, if we can dissociate ourselves from the constant stream of thoughts—*in our own mind*—we can find lasting peace in the present moment! For me, along with thousands of other Eckhart Tolle fans, I would soon learn, this struck a huge chord. The idea to me was so simple, yet so profound. And Tolle has a gift of presenting his ideas clearly and interestingly. I was truly moved by *The Power of Now*.

Though I wasn't aware of it at the time, this moment in my life—stumbling onto *The Power of Now*—marked the beginning of my formal spiritual journey. And I am so grateful for it. For it was after reading that book that a fire was lit within me to learn more. Shortly after reading that book, the thought occurred to me, *Well, if this one book has such profound insight, what about all these other spiritual books? What do they all have to say?* And so, to put it simply, I went on a book-binging tear. I dove headfirst into those racks for the next twelve to eighteen months.

I bought and read book after book, and I loved all the teachings and concepts in them. There was information about angels, spirit guides, the divine feminine, divine guidance, God, the goddess, spirit, and a host of related topics. And I was in a truly fortunate position. I knew God was real, because of the Revelation, so maybe all these other spiritual ideas and beings existed, too. I couldn't get enough of these teachings from these lovely books. Could I remember any more than around two and a half percent of what I read? Ah, no. But I loved reading them anyway. Reading them gave me a sense of comfort and joy. And I was learning rather quickly that there is a whole new world, or a way of looking at the world, that I was not aware of before.

Again, I wasn't aware of it during this pivotal period, but I was turning into a metaphysical, spiritual-minded person. A few pages back, I wrote about my observation that there are two kinds of people in the world —those who are materially oriented and those who are spiritually oriented. I'm not saying one is better than, or superior to, the other; I believe everyone is perfect where they are now. I'm just saying that is what I have observed. I believe everyone in the world is on the spiritual path, but it's just that most are not aware of it. So as I plowed through the religion and spirituality section, I myself was making the transition, or rather transformation, from the materially focused to the spiritually oriented. And it was great.

Though this transformation took on a formal nature (seeking knowledge through books, then eventually conferences and retreats), I don't actually know when the transition really started. For a period of years, beginning just after The Plunge in 1997, I had been secretly following "signs" and "synchronicities," as I called them.

The first thing I can remember doing on intuition alone was picking up and reading the angel book I mentioned.

That was just after I was released from the hospital. Truth be told, that was the first of many, many times I would see a "sign" or experience a synchronicity, and follow it. This was long before I encountered any of the books I found in Barnes & Noble on how to ask for and follow spiritual guidance. I just began to follow signs. There did not seem to be rhyme or reason to my choices, and I didn't consciously know anything about spirituality or spiritual guidance. Naturally, I told *no one* what I was doing. I'm sure my friends and family thought I was crazy enough after The Plunge—no need to add on.

By the time I discovered modern spiritual teachers like Sonia Choquette, Dr. Wayne Dyer, and Deepak Chopra, I was an old pro at following "prompts" or guidance. Take, for instance, when I quit drinking back in 2000. I just *knew* it was no coincidence when mom did that one-person intervention on me *the day after* my Lynette humiliation, so I followed her suggestion to quit drinking and went to rehab. Thirteen years later, in 2013, while parked in our Gun Bun gravel parking lot, I was asking my higher self (my intuition) if I should return to work at the winery. Just then, Jeff drove around the corner in his big white Nissan pickup truck and extended a friendly wave to me as he drove by. Well, that sign was good enough for me! I decided to go back to work for the family right then.

In truth, there are probably hundreds of examples like these—asking what to do, waiting for a sign or intuition, then following it—that occurred over the years after The

Plunge. I know I'm not alone in this sort of experience. In fact, it was in 2006, during my trip through the spirituality section of Barnes & Noble, that I learned that I was *not* the only one in the world who "follows signs." It turns out there are thousands upon thousands of people around the world who are "crazy" just like me, who are into spirituality, following divine guidance, and such similar practices. It is called the New Age movement. Now *I* was officially part of the New Age movement. Not bad. The time I spent in Florida at Barnes & Noble, sipping coffee and reading all those books about God and everything else under the sun, are some of my fondest memories.

I feel I should interject here that, though I have followed and do follow guidance, or intuition, it is only intermittent, and not always accurate. And I realize that not consistently asking Spirit for guidance, and then following it, is a main obstacle to my achieving permanent peace of mind. I can't overstate how often I repeat the advice to myself that I *must* make a constant habit of asking, then *listening* for an answer. This is one of the main messages of *A Course in Miracles*—to make contact with the Holy Spirit within, and turn to Him for guidance on how to perceive something that is troubling us. He will then help us change our perception, or perform a miracle, and bring peace. I'm nowhere near perfect at this, but I am constantly working on it.

I can't talk about my time at Barnes & Noble without mentioning Dave. I love Dave. Dave was a regular customer at the store. He was a little older than I was, a bit portly, and he had lost the fight to keep his hair long ago. Over time, he and I developed a friendship. Dave had a big mind and loved to talk about all things philosophical. Right up my alley. It wasn't long after I met him that I learned that he was a staunch atheist. He didn't just not believe in God, but he had devoted his life to proving to himself that there was no God. He shared that he had a huge library in his basement, literally racks and racks of books filled with knowledge. Now imagine running into me!

Obviously, I took the other position with regard to God. And so over time Dave and I debated — in a friendly manner— the merits of our respective positions. I don't remember the specifics of what he or I said. I'm pretty sure I did not share with him my revelation experience. What I do know is that I did not evangelize. I had no personal interest in changing his mind. What he chose to believe was none of my business. I still go by this philosophy today. I think Dave appreciated that I never tried to "convert" him to anything. I just shared my own experience, strength, and hope (to borrow a phrase from AA), and left it at that. Which is why we were able to continue our conversations every time he came into the store.

On one of our last encounters before I quit Barnes & Noble, as I prepared to move back to California, Dave gave me one of the best compliments I've ever gotten. He said, "You know, I have to give you credit. You're the first person I've ever met who's given me a bit of a pause. You've got me thinking."

As far as I knew, I'd never gotten anyone thinking about anything, so it felt pretty good. It was a great way to end my time at the big store.

There's one more thing I'd like to mention. One day, while I was scanning books in the religion and spirituality section, I felt prompted to pick up and look at a curious title. It had a blue cover and was big and thick and heavy. This book had some meat to it; it was a real lunker. The title on the cover was *A Course in Miracles*. I knew nothing about it, besides a vague memory of someone mentioning it at an AA meeting. I opened the book, flipped to a random page, and began to read.

After just a few sentences, I was like, "What the hell is this?" I had no idea what it was saying. It may as well have been written in Chinese. I said to myself, "Ah, no." Then I tucked the book quickly back on the shelf. I must have been attracted to the thick blue book, though, because I repeated this exercise once or twice more later on, and ended up with the same result. "Ah, no."

So ran my thinking at the time.

THIRTY

Spiritual Seeking Continued...

IN LATE 2006, my therapist announced to me out of the blue that she was moving away, back to her home state up north. With that news—that I would no longer be working with her—it occurred to me that I had no other real purpose for being in south Florida. My illicit relationship had effectively ended the year before. I hadn't seen or spoken to her for over a year, besides a run-in at the bagel shop. Though I enjoyed my job at Barnes & Noble, it wasn't a reason to stick around. Looking back, it seems it was time to shift out of my therapeutic relationship and move into another phase of my journey.

Again, I did not consciously plan this big change. But after what would come, it sure seems as if there was a Higher Power involved in the orchestration of my life. And besides, it just felt right that it was time to return home. So I packed my bags, said goodbye to my small handful of AA friends, loaded Bull and Nonie into the back seat of my truck along with all my other things, and set off on the long drive up the Florida coast and across the USA, back to California, back to where it all began.

As the saying goes, "The more things change, the more they stay the same." I ended up landing in Davis, California, the college town from where I had set off on this wild adventure after high school. I found an apartment and went to work on starting a small one-man business— a window-cleaning service. I called it Squeaky Clean Window Washing. I visited family. Got together with my old college friends for a round or two of golf and Texas Hold 'em.

I continued to go to AA meetings in my new town, but like in Florida, I generally kept to myself. But the habit I continued that meant the most to me, my vocation so to speak, was to hang in bookstores, reading spiritual books. I couldn't get enough. This time the site of my book searches and reading was the local Davis Borders Bookstore—sadly, now a defunct business.

One title I specifically remember reading and really enjoying was *Autobiography of a Yogi* by Paramahansa Yogananda. The one characteristic of Paramahansa that I deeply admired was his unflinching devotion to God and to his Guru, who was his spiritual guide. He had a light way that he seemed to go through his life, a sort of flow, that I loved and admired. I wished as I read his life story that I was as devoted as he was. But I knew I was not.

For instance, Paramahansa was completely devoted to God and the spiritual journey, and (if I remember correctly) he never mentioned anything about being attracted to women (or men). I couldn't help but wonder how he avoided that? But anyway, the significant part of this little story is that *I* was admiring someone completely devoted to God! Now how did that happen? Obviously, given all that I'd been through, a change had been taking place in my mind, even if I was not wholly aware of it. In fact, my whole outlook on life, the world, people, and myself had begun to transform since I'd stumbled onto spirituality just a few short years ago.

By this time, in 2007 in Davis, as I mentioned above, I was quietly part of the New Age movement. I had attempted to follow exercises from various spiritual teachers and teachings. For a time, for instance, I was really into a little pink book called *Angel Numbers* by Doreen Virtue. According to that book, there is a spiritual message behind numbers given by angels. So if you see specific numbers out in the world, like 1:11 on a clock, for instance, those numbers have a specific message for you.

Being a big fan of looking for signs, I now saw numbers all over the place, and I have to confess that often a specific message, or number, came at just the right time to make me feel better. For instance, one day I remember walking through a parking lot in Davis, lost in thought, troubled about something, when I saw the number 222 on a license plate. Then I remembered, according to the book, the message for the number 222 is essentially, "Don't worry about a thing! Everything is working out for everyone involved." In effect, practicing with the little book helped introduce healing thoughts into the clutter of ego thoughts that I was normally immersed in. In fact, using ideas from many of the spiritual books I had found often helped me feel better—but only temporarily. Because before long, I would be right back into being immersed in fear or guilt-based ego thoughts.

Speaking of the ego, though I have mentioned the ego a few times, I have not shared much about it. Before my journey officially started, before The Plunge, back in my early days, I knew about as much about the ego as anyone else. I'd heard things like, "He has a big ego." Or "She is so full of herself." I, on the other hand, didn't think I had an ego. Ha! Talk about denial!

In college, I took one or two psych classes and learned about Sigmund Freud and Carl Jung, among others. I certainly was no expert, but I learned a bit about ego, superego, id, behaviorism and such concepts. Actually, come to think of it, I also took an abnormal psych class. I had absolutely no idea at the time that I would, a few short years later, become a *subject* in that field! Anyway, in short, I had an average understanding of this concept of ego, and beyond that, I never paid much attention to it. As it tuns out, after being on the spiritual journey for a little while, I learned that an average understanding of the ego comes *way, way* short of what the ego truly is.

If there was one thing that came up consistently in many of the spiritual books I looked at or read, it is the ego. Besides God, the ego is the common theme in spirituality. To be more specific, it is commonly taught throughout most if not all spiritualities that the ego is the main obstacle to peace for all humanity. It is the main adversary. This is the general message I got from reading all those spiritual books —that though all our problems in life seem to be outside us—bills to pay, bad grades, divorce, the economy, a loved one's death, crime and now, in 2021—a pandemic—in truth, all our problems are actually *within* us, in the form of the ego. *It is the ego within that is the real problem in the world—the great adversary.*

But still the question is—what is the ego? It's a decidedly abstract idea, and many teachers I encountered in my travels to the bookstore have tried explaining it in different ways, and I don't think there is actually a definitive answer, so I'm not going to attempt to describe it. I'm just bringing it up because sometime in early 2007, when I was in Davis, I figured out what my real problem was: my ego. Eventually the question dawned on me: *what would be the best way to overcome, or transcend, this ego thing?* That, in effect, is what all of these teachers were getting at.

I feel I should note that for a brief time, before I became more aware of the ego problem, I got caught up in perhaps the most popular pastime in the New Age movement: manifesting things. There are dozens of books in the New Age section that help people learn how to use their mind and their thoughts to manifest whatever they want in the world, like a new job, or a new romantic relationship, or perhaps the most widespread, a parking spot! Arguably, the most popular modern book on the subject is called *The Secret*.

Thus, for a period of time, I read *The Secret*, along with other similar books. I made vision boards, where I pasted pictures of vegetables (I ate a lot of junk food), a book cover for envisioning my first book, and a married couple with a picture of my face pasted over the male model's, leaving my potential partner's face blank, since I didn't know who she would be. The idea was that if I thought about these things, visualized them in my mind, they would manifest in my life sometime in the future.

Anyway, I played with manifestation ideas for a while, until later, after doing more research (meaning: being led to the right books and teachers), it started to become clearer to me that getting things would not solve my problems. Even if I ate better, published a book, and got married, I'd still be stuck with me! And that is a problem.

As I mentioned above, I came to understand that the ego in me was the real problem, not my eating habits or lack of girlfriend, and it was this alone that I needed to deal with. This was another gift of The Plunge—it was always in the back of my mind. And so, deep down, healing that experience was always an unmentioned but top priority for me. It eventually became pretty obvious that The Plunge had something to do with the ego. The only question was, who, what, where, when and how would I get the help I needed to undo this little adversary in me?

These were the thoughts and ideas running around in the back of my mind, like ingredients stirring around in a big pot. They swirled around while I was working my new window-cleaning business, which is a great job for getting lost in thought. And they showed up while I was hanging at the Davis Borders Bookstore. What was becoming a more and more common experience, Spirit didn't take long to address.

THIRTY-ONE

Stumbling onto
A Course in Miracles

I T WAS just another day in Davis. I had time on my hands, as usual, so I went over to Borders to have some coffee, maybe get a burger at the restaurant next door, and peruse the books again. It was sometime in 2007, and by now my impassioned nosedive into spiritual searching and book reading was beginning to wind down. I'd found and read, or at least looked at, most of the books I had an interest in.

I'd come to understand the ego problem, but I didn't overtly tell myself, "I'm going to find a way to undo the ego today," or anything like that. I just came to the book store to casually look at books while I got my daily fix of caffeine, grease and sugar. As I scanned the stacks, I saw many titles I was familiar with, including one I'd seen once or twice before, but had for some reason ignored. This time, though, I plucked it off the shelf and read the cover.

The book was called *The Disappearance of the Universe* by Gary R. Renard. For some reason, I love titles. I often try to think of new titles for imaginary books I would write someday. It's kind of an obsession. Anyway, I thought this title was an intriguing one. The idea of the universe disappearing had never occurred to me before. It seems so permanent. Then I read the subtitle of the book: *Straight Talk about Illusions, Past Lives, Religion, Sex, Politics, and the Miracles of Forgiveness.* What was this? It was not often that sex was so overtly mixed in with spiritual teachings, or at least not the ones I'd encountered. The author had my attention. So I took the book over to the cafe area of the bookstore, found an empty chair, and sat down to give it a read.

I'll be damned. Or saved, as the case may be! This was it. This was the big one. The Big Kahuna. Not far into this book, I felt kind of excited, and very delighted. After reading not too far into the book, I felt that I might have found what I didn't even know I was looking for. And what a game changer it turned out to be. The author has a great sense of humor, and the content of his book was/ is unbelievable!

As it turns out, this book was all about *A Course in Miracles*, even though it doesn't mention it by name on the cover. The book is formatted as a conversation between three people; Gary and two ascended masters named Arten and Pursah, who happened to appear out of thin air on Gary's couch one day as he sat in his living room meditating. I know—sounds kind of hard to believe. But considering I'm claiming I've been to both hell and Heaven, who would I be, not to believe Gary? And besides, as they—Arten and Pursah—point out in the book, it's not about the messengers anyway, but the message. And it is a doozy.

Yes, yes, yes. That's all I could think as I read D.U. (as Gary's many readers refer to *The Disappearance of the Universe*). His book, in a very entertaining and humorous manner, goes on to explain what the message of *A Course in Miracles* actually is. After reading his book, I bought a copy of the Course, and immediately began to study. And God-not-forbid, I actually had a clue of what the heck the Course was talking about, and it was a miracle. No more Chinese for me. Anyway, after reading D.U. and beginning with the Course, it dawned on me that I had found a path, and possibly *the* path that I never knew I was looking for. And it was all because of Gary's book!

Not long after I had found D.U. and the Course, I attended a conference at Hay House, which is a popular publisher of modern spiritual texts. Gary was one of the presenters. I brought my D.U. copy along and asked him to sign it after his presentation. He was kind and patient with me, and seemed genuinely pleased after I stammered out nervously my gratitude that his book had been instrumental to my finding the Course — even though no doubt he'd heard this story a thousand times before. Besides the Course, there is no book I have read more times than Gary's. Every time I seemed to slack off with the Course for a period of time, I'd pick up my copy of D.U., start reading, and go, *Oh yeah, that's why I became a Course student.* D.U. has gotten me back on track more than once. You can hardly find his signature anymore, what with all the colorful highlights and notes scribbled throughout my copy. And so, stumbling onto the right book, at the right time, after a lot of trial and error, was the way that I found what would become my path home.

THIRTY-TWO

Follower

The Holy Spirit will always guide you truly,
because your joy is His.
This is His Will for everyone
because He speaks for the Kingdom of God,
which is joy.
Following Him is therefore the easiest thing in the world,
and the only thing that **is** *easy,*
because it is not of the world.
—A Course in Miracles T-7.XI.1:1-3

Just because I found D.U. and *A Course in Miracles*—and was very excited about it—doesn't mean I immediately and blindly became a Course student. I deeply wanted to be *guided* to find and choose the right path. And so, I wanted to follow the way that was right for me. Below, I share a story about my thoughts on "following" and how it affected my life, and how it ultimately helped me to make the right choice for me.

One day, when I was around eleven years old, I was walking down our long driveway, which winds its way through our rolling La Paz vineyard. I don't remember where I was headed, maybe to Ricardo and Harvey's house, or the school bus stop. As I walked, I was thinking about my relationships. In particular, I was thinking about my relationships with the males in my life.

As I reviewed my relationships with my dad, my older brother Jeff, and even my then-best friend Jon, it was crystal clear to me that I took a subordinate role to all of them. I noted that all of them had characteristics of the alpha personality, or leadership traits, while I clearly was a beta personality, or a follower (I'm not so sure I used those terms at eleven years old, but I was thinking those ideas in some form as I understood back then).

As I have noted in other parts of this book, when Dad said "Jump," I said, "How high?" Jeff clearly was the dominant one between us older siblings. And Jon simply is and always has been a natural leader. I observed this as I walked, and I noted that I am nothing like them. I did not have these traits and *knew* (at the time) I could never develop them. I understood I was the opposite.

Walking down the lane that day, I consciously decided to accept that "I am a follower." I knew there was nothing I could do to change it. It was just a simple fact. And so I made this declaration to myself. And that was that.

But it did not come without a cost.

By the time I was having these thoughts, I knew on an intuitive level our American culture's general attitude about leaders and followers. Being an ambitious, fearless, hard-charging authoritative leader, in general, is regarded as "good." That is what people should strive to be. An image of the rugged, strong, individual Marlboro Man comes to mind. Or my dad or Grandpa Cannon or Great-great-Grandma Martha Hughes Cannon, for that matter. And if one couldn't be that, he might consider making changes until he does become a leader.

Conversely, the "weaker," timid, unconfident, beta follower personality is regarded as "bad," or at least less than. I don't necessarily know how my classmates or people outside me perceived me, but inside I felt like and *knew* I was the latter: a timid, unconfident follower, through and through. I cannot overstate how much I crucified myself inside over the years of my youth for being like this: weak inside, afraid to share my voice (unless I was drunk—a few years later), timid and alone.

Yes, there were moments here and there where I displayed some leadership qualities. Like the time in second grade when I decided to take on the class bully in a fight (and lost). Or like the time one of our Babe Ruth baseball coaches encouraged us underaged players to drink beer at practice. Wanting to win more than to drink (at the time), and being an elder on the team, I rebelled against the coach and convinced about half the team to come join me for a side practice, while the rest of the team drank beer with the coach. Or the times I stood on the pitcher's mound of the baseball diamond. I played pitcher from little league through high school. A baseball pitcher is a leadership position of a sort, at least at those levels. But overall, with regard to the personal relationships in my life, I felt like the follower.

The ego in me showed no mercy. No mercy at all. I was hard on myself for my own inner perceived weaknesses. In fact, I crucified myself inwardly often over my weak personality, not to mention every time I didn't say or do the right thing. Or when I failed to do something perfectly. I (ego) was truly brutal on myself. The only evidence I can point to that demonstrates how brutal the ego in me was on me, is to point to The Plunge as a result of the savage mental pounding that I took within. I have joked to myself that I am the reverse-Adolf Hitler: meaning what would it look like if someone projected as much hatred as Hitler did outwardly, inwardly towards their own self? Answer: me.

Please note I am quite aware that I am *not* alone in my tendency toward self-loathing. We all experience self-loathing to one degree or another. As the Course would eventually point out to me, it is the human condition. Also, I am obviously not the only "follower" personality in the world. We are all in this together.

Much of my self-loathing seemed to come from my perception of myself as a beta "follower" personality. Put simply, I believed being a follower was bad. I was a follower. Therefore, I was bad.

Imagine my surprise, then, many years down the road, when I learned that the world is upside-down and that being a follower is not such a bad thing after all. It all depends on who you follow.

Looking back, my tendency to follow seemed to turn

in a positive, healing direction when I surrendered in Mom's kitchen and decided to get help for my drinking. Before that, I seemed to be completely under the control of the ego, and followed its dictates almost perfectly. When its voice told me to say yes to someone or something, when in my heart I wanted to say a hard no, I almost always said yes. And vice versa. I often did another's will at the expense of my own inner joy and peace. This is commonly called people-pleasing, and I seemed to take it to the next level.

And when it came to self-destruction, I was also a loyal follower of the ego. Its guidance was to have another drink or hit, and another one after that, *it won't hurt.* Go ahead, skip class, *no one cares anyway.* I once spent an entire semester at USF skipping class during the entire school week, for instance, until I could go out drinking with my friends on the weekend. Every day, I lay on my bed reading the Rex Stout mystery novels my grandmother Betty Cannon had turned me on to. Did this create a *ton* of guilt in me? It sure did, but I just stuffed it all down, as usual. I was not an expert at anything in life, I imagine, save one: following the ego. (ACIM teaches that we *all* are experts at this, or we wouldn't be here.)

But finally that all turned around when I heard another voice in me that day mom did her intervention, the same voice that told me to run during The Plunge, and I followed it instead. This brings up a topic I'd like to share, which I learned from *A Course in Miracles.*

Like the vast majority of people in the world, I grew

up with the belief and experience that there was only one voice in my mind. This voice spoke for a vast array of ideas and beliefs that I had built up in my mind since the day I was born. This vast array of beliefs and ideas developed into my personality and my own personal truths, my own personal view on the world and on my self—my body, intellect, abilities, etc. The Course summarizes this self we each make as the self-concept. And this self-concept is built up largely by listening to and following this little voice in my mind that keeps a running commentary. It (what the Course calls the ego), is always *yakking*; judging, analyzing, perceiving, commenting on things around us and in us. I think most people get this. We all have this little voice in our mind, and we are convinced it is us. This surely is how I grew up. Listening to this voice, believing in it faithfully, following it.

This is all great and good, but according to the Course (and my own personal experience), there is one little problem. This voice (of the ego) is mad (crazy). I think the story of my life chronicled in this book is a great example of how mad the ego is.

It is far less commonly known that there is *another* voice in our mind that most of us are not even aware of. Though I believe most have heard or seen reference to it many, many times in popular culture as well as in our own life. Think "our better angels" of Abraham Lincoln or "Use the Force, Luke," from Obi-Wan Kenobi in *Star Wars*, or that time you felt an intuitive feeling to call a friend, and when you did, you learned she was in trouble and really needed to hear from you. The point is, *A Course in Miracles* reveals that there *really* is another voice in our mind, and this voice is not of this world, but is of God, Who is within us. Forgive me for bringing in the "G" Word here, but I have to share about this, as it pertains to me being a "follower."

ABOUT A YEAR before I found ACIM, I had learned of this other voice during my spiritual journey to the bookstores. The authors I read gave it names like Inner Guide, or Spiritual Guide. The main point they all made was that this inner voice is actually real, and not a figment of my imagination. In general, all the various authors suggested you learn to "hear" this Inner Guide, then follow it. See what happens. Eventually, I found *A Course in Miracles*, and it, too, taught of this Inner Guide. It calls this Inner Guide the Holy Spirit. And the Course suggests one learn to ask for guidance and follow it.

In short, I was more than happy to try this "following Inner Guidance" thing. Way more than happy. I had been following authority figures (teachers, parents, etc.) all my life, not to mention my own "worse angels" within. All I got was loss, terror, and loads and loads of guilt, along with a constant mild depression. Why not give it up, see if there really is a Higher Authority in there, in my mind? What the Heaven?

In retrospect, it didn't take much time for me to see that I had actually done a pretty darn good job of following this Holy Spirit in my past, even though I had no clue it was Him I was following. These "better angels" within had guided me to quit drinking, move to Florida, work with a therapist, study spirituality, return to California, and find and practice (or follow) ACIM. Not bad.

I did not know I was following an Inner Guide, but indeed I was. Only after I found the Course (and spirituality in general) did I really begin to understand and *believe* that there is a *real*, Inner Guide in there, and that It or He has my best interest at heart. According to the Course (and my own experience), this Inner Guide, or Holy Spirit, is deep and still and quiet. Being a communication link between God, Who is also real, and me here in this world, this voice for love only has my best interest at heart. This voice is all about love, and only love. Now what could be wrong with that? As the quote at the top of this chapter alludes to, this Inner Guide's sole purpose is our (or my) joy. It wants us to be happy, *really* happy, plain and simple. And I can attest that having consciously followed this "other voice" now for over ten years (though definitely not perfectly), happiness, or inner peace, really is its goal for me.

And so I have learned, at last, that "following" — if one finds the right authority figure to follow — is actually a "good" ability to have. In the right-side-up world, I actually have a good ability — the ability to follow my Inner Guide.

And I would put this newfound ability to use, as I needed to find and follow guidance when I was confronted with perhaps the most important choice of my life.

THIRTY-THREE

The Choice

AT ABOUT the same time I stumbled onto D.U. and the Course, I also was looking at other spiritual studies. In particular, I was looking at disciplines that would help rid me of that little devil inside me called the ego. For instance, I looked at Paramahansa Yogananda's Kriya Yoga. Kriya Yoga is an ancient meditation technique of energy and breath control, or pranayama. It is part of a comprehensive spiritual path. This means that it concerns itself with helping a practitioner to overcome the ego and achieve enlightenment, as all authentic spiritual paths are designed to do. I looked into this pretty seriously, and even sent away for some pamphlets and materials to learn more.

At the same time, I found another internationally well-known Eastern mystical teacher and healer named Amma, or Mata Amritanandamayi. Amma is known around the world as "the hugging saint," and she has traveled the world for decades, hugging millions of her followers as well as anyone in need of healing and love. For anyone willing, she also offers a comprehensive spiritual path. I was really drawn to Amma. I felt a draw toward the divine feminine, and was attracted to her Mother energy. I learned that she has a California ashram not more than an hour or two from Davis, and I looked her up on the internet to see when she would be in California next.

As it turned out, Amma came to California quite often. She has a big following here, as well as in other countries all over the world. I went to her ashram and was blown away. Tucked into the rolling hills about an hour east of San Francisco on the outskirts of the town of San Ramon, it is a beautiful property. Surrounded by wild oaks and golden grass, the ashram sits atop a small incline. It is a large building that, when full, must seat over a thousand people. Two stories high and made of wood, it has tall ceilings and smells of incense and fresh flowers. There is even room for a bookstore and shop, with all things Amma and her teachings. Above the ashram and adjacent to it, there are gardens where they harvest vegetables used to serve the guests when they arrive to see Amma and get a blessing and a hug from her. Yet beyond all the beauty of the property, nothing compared to Amma herself.

She is amazing. To see her tirelessly extend love to all who come to see her, words cannot describe Amma. Her mission is to give a hug and blessing to anyone who comes to see her. One of the days I visited, the ashram was full, and it literally took all day, all night, and into the next morning for her to hug everyone who was there.

There were three separate long lines of people waiting to kneel before her. Or maybe it was four. Watching her interact with and bless each and every individual in the building, I knew I couldn't last twenty minutes doing what she was doing. Clearly, Spirit was working through her, as she seemed to be in a constant state of joy and compassion. If I remember correctly, her disciples shared that after the Satsang (a spiritual discourse or sacred gathering) is over—we're talking fifteen to twenty hours straight—Amma will then cook breakfast the next morning for all her disciples and helpers who helped her through the night. Wow. After visiting her, joining with her and getting my hug (!), I believe she is a spiritually enlightened being.

I seriously considered becoming a follower of Amma, and choosing her way as my path. I went so far as to get a mantra from her—a secret prayer she gives to people who want to become a disciple. Among other directions, the mantra she gives is meant to be told to *no one*. It is a prayer shared only with the divine, and it is meant to be my own direct link to Amma, and ultimately to God. Every time I invoke my mantra, she will be there with me. I have never told my mantra to anyone. And I have to say, I have used it in some very difficult times, and it has brought great comfort. Thus, I was very close to pushing in all my chips with Amma and becoming a disciple of hers.

But there was this other, less well-known, less tested, seemingly more radical, newer path that involved a blue-covered book with gold letters and the fantastic claim that the author is Jesus. I couldn't forget about that. For as I was visiting with Amma, I was also continuing to read and learn the Course. In the end, it came down to Amma or Jesus (ACIM). I considered both, and was not certain which path was right for me. So I did (amazingly) what both Amma and the Course would suggest their students do—I asked for guidance. I asked Spirit, "Which path is right for me?" Then I waited for an answer.

Sadly, I only have a vague recollection of what form my guidance took. There is a memory of seeing a physical sign at a spirituality conference I attended that same year that had something to do with my guidance. Also, sometime early on in my journey with the Course, I read about a powerful vision the Course's scribe, Dr. Helen Schucman, had. In the vision she encountered the word "Evoe" which describes the rites of Bacchus (god of grape-growing and winemaking), along with the word "Elohim," a Hebrew name for God. Well, Bacchus also happens to be the name we used to market Gun Bun wines for many years in our company's history. And it is the current name of our wine club: The Bacchus Club. For me, this was no coincidence. That is about what I can remember. And I'd say Jesus visiting me in a dream where I am lifted into Heaven played into my decision, too. All I can say is that whatever my guidance was, it was crystal clear that I was to become a Course student. And so I did. *A Course in Miracles* is my path. Jesus in the house! Amen...

Amma forgives me.

THIRTY-FOUR

My Dream Comes True

W HAT IS *A Course in Miracles*? Well, many have tried to answer this question, but it's hard to define. In general, I'd say it is a purely non-dual authentic spiritual path. It is meant to help its students undo the ego and return their mind to wholeness. This is accomplished by a student's practice of a special form of forgiveness. And it is also accomplished by the student's learning of the Holy Spirit (or what some would call our Inner Guide), and turning to Him for guidance in healing our mind, correcting our perception, or as the Course teaches, performing a miracle.

When the goal of the Course is achieved, the student will awaken to the innate Spirit or Light that is in them, that *is* them, and then they will be unconditionally happy. It is a way to happiness. In fact, I could write twenty pages on the Course, what it is, and why I love it so much. And I did! I have added my description of the Course in an appendix at the back of the book, for anyone who is interested in learning more about it. I will only say that it is the way for me, simply because it has brought me so much peace and joy.

The Plunge even to this day (July 2021), still lingers at the back of my mind. It's not uncommon for a blip of fear to come up in relation to The Plunge, even though I am a dedicated Course student now.

And though the purpose of the Course is broad in its application, each of us finds our way to dealing with personal issues using the context and content of the Course. For example, for me, once I had a deeper understanding of the Course, I could clearly see that The Plunge was an hallucination, a dream. In fact, this is one of the main ways in which *A Course in Miracles* helps to dispel illusions. Added to that is the way in which the Course speaks so authoritatively about revelation, which made it the perfect course for me.

I can also say confidently that I believe my whole life, from my drinking to get lit, to The Plunge, to the long, windy spiritual journey that I ended up on, was to get me *finally* to *A Course in Miracles*. Remember, getting rid of that little devil the ego, which for me includes my memory of The Plunge, became my only ambition. And for me, the Course is the way. There are many other ways, of course, and they may appeal to others. Yet I love the Course to no end because it presents what I believe is the quickest way to dispel the ego, and let the light that is in me, that *is* me, shine into awareness. That, happily, is it.

After finding *A Course in Miracles* and becoming one of its students in 2007 in Davis, I knew, as I shared above, that I had found the way. I would begin to study daily, read its text and begin its workbook. While I worked with the Course directly, I also spent my free time Googling about the Course, its various teachers, communities, and other related information.

I would learn there is a Course community based in San Francisco called Community Miracles Center, that not only meets to study and celebrate the Course, but hosts an annual Course conference every year somewhere around the U.S. Consisting of around five hundred like-minded people and lots of good food, good spirits, and lovely teachers and workshops, the two conferences I ended up attending were a remarkable experience, and I truly enjoyed myself at both. I also spent time at a Course-inspired monastery in Utah called Living Miracles, where I learned from the prominent teacher, David Hoffmeister. And I would even join a Course group, as I mentioned earlier.

Thus, my life after 2007 became all about the Course, and I cannot overstate how much peace and joy this new way of life had given me. Yet, I also continued to live my normal life and pursue my other personal goals and desires as well.

After living in Davis for around three years, I decided to move back to Sonoma in 2010, into a converted downstairs apartment at my mother's house. I continued my window-washing business for a time, before eventually deciding (after asking for guidance) to go back to work at Gun Bun as a tour guide in 2013. I still loved to go to the movies, I spent a lot of time in coffeeshops and bookstores, and I had also begun writing my first book, *Enlighten-ment Everyone*. And yet, though I had found my way with the Course, I hadn't let go of my old heart's desire to find a partner to share my life.

Being a Course student, I learned what I believe to be the most valuable lesson of all. Namely, that this world teaches us to search for love and satisfaction *outside* our-selves in all the things and people of the world—fame, for-tune, a special love relationship, a big promotion at work, the approval of others, a new car, a new job, a new house, the next special love relationship (after our first ended painfully), a diamond ring, a trip to Jamaica, concert tick-ets to see a favorite artist, a big win in anything—sports, politics, business, over an adversary. And on and on it goes. And as part of this lesson, this world also teaches us that when we get these things and people we desire, we will be "saved" or find peace, or be happy. Nope!

The Course, along with all authentic spiritual paths, teaches the most valuable lesson of all: the true love and sense of power, glory, freedom and abundance that we all so deeply desire is actually wholly in the *opposite* di-rection—it is directly inward, at the very center of our own being. True love and everything we ever wanted, including peace of mind, is *within*, and *only* there will any of us, including me, ever find it.*

*Note: the Course does not necessarily advocate you give up the things of the world. One can buy a house or be famous, for instance. It merely asks you to ask for guid-ance, and remain unattached to the things of the world, even as you enjoy them.

And yet... after learning this and even understanding it to a degree, I still held on to hope that I would find a beloved partner to spend my life with. As it turns out, that's not a problem. With Spirit, one can have their cake and eat it, too.

For a couple of years, between 2010 and 2012, I became friends with a couple of lovely young women in Sonoma. Though I was not exactly dating them, it seemed like there was possibility with each of them. But for whatever reason, or various reasons, those relationships never went further than friendship. But I still held on to my hope, and eventually even took a little action. I asked the Holy Spirit for help.

It's Sunday, June 17th 2012, Father's Day, and the Bundschus are out on a family bike ride. It's a beautiful day, sunny, not too hot, and lots of blue sky and golden grass dancing in the breeze along the hillsides surrounding our little town of Sonoma. We are riding along the country backroads winding just east of downtown, and we are celebrating Dad today with this leisurely bike ride, which will be followed by a family dinner on the back porch of Jeff, Liz and the girls' house back in town. About halfway through the ride, out of the blue, Jeff casually mentions to me, "Hey Rob, just wanted to give you a heads up that we invited our new neighbor over for dinner with us tonight. She seems very friendly and appears to be single, and she's around your age. We're not trying to set you up or anything (wink, wink), but we just wanted to let you know." This bit of news certainly perked me up a little.

I had recently written a one-page note to Spirit, asking to meet my life partner. I listed a few qualities that I hoped she would have, including that she be beautiful, loving, down to earth, loves to stop to smell the roses, spiritual (but doesn't necessarily have to be a Course student), and perhaps most importantly, is accepting of me and my crazy past as well as my relatively new devotion to the Course and my forgiveness practice. I made sure to add, "or someone better" at the end of my note, in order to acknowledge that I still may not know what is best for me, and that Spirit does.

None of this was on my mind as I sat in my chair at the dinner table outside on the patio that night, quietly waiting for our special guest to arrive. The family was already gathered there, around the table, when she came walking out the back door, carrying a lovely dish she had prepared for the occasion.

My first thought was how beautiful she was, with her long flowing hair, her warm smile, and the easy, natural way she entered our little world there in the back yard. And then I couldn't help but admire how brave she was for joining our family at a meal even though she barely knew any of us.

She sat next to me, and I spent most of the evening looking at her, but trying not to be too obvious about it. And I quietly listened as she shared about her background, where she was from, how she came to be in Sonoma, and her stories of adventures from around Europe and the world. She spoke with a lovely accent, which we learned came from her Turkish heritage, where she had been born and raised. By the end of the evening, I was enchanted, and all I knew was that I hoped I would see her again.

As we were heading for the front door on our way out, we agreed to exchange emails and meet soon. And sure enough, Zeynep and I did meet for coffee a few days later. And then we went on our first date, out to a great little Mexican restaurant in town. And the rest, as they say, is history.

My dream had come true at last.

After a long and lovely courtship, Zeynep and I were happily married at the winery with all our family and friends surrounding us on a warm Friday evening, June 30th, 2017. There was delicious food, plenty of good wine flowing (for everyone else), endless dancing, and most of all, lots of love flowing around and through us all. It was truly a night of miracles. Spirit had answered the prayer of my heart, and brought to me someone who was everything I had ever wanted, and yet "someone even better."

I love you, always and forever.

THIRTY-FIVE

A Shot at Writing

I T'S EARLY 2016, and I am standing before a room full of family and friends and Zeynep, who was my girl friend at the time. There are perhaps thirty or forty people in total, and I am nervous. It's nine years since I had returned to California from Florida, and six years since I'd moved back to Sonoma from Davis. We are all gathered in the Bungalow on Rhinefarm. The big day has finally arrived. Today is the official launch of my new book and program, called *Enlightenment Everyone: Thirteen Steps To Finding Your True Self.*

I began writing the book back in 2009 in Davis. After having been a Course student for a couple years, I decided to take being "a savior of the world" literally. In short, I had found so much peace on the spiritual path that I wanted to create a way for others to launch their own spiritual journey. And that way was to create a step program loosely based on twelve-step recovery programs. And here I was, in the Bungalow, ready to give a talk on spirituality and the story of the inspiration for my book to those close to me. It was nerve-wracking, since I had a habit of keeping my spiritual thoughts and stories to myself.

I used a reproduction of a Vincent van Gogh painting, *Starry Night over the Rhone*, on the cover of my new book, because I felt a particular affinity with Vincent—we had led similar lives, in my judgement. As it turns out, my proselytizing for Spirit went about as well as it did for Vincent, when he briefly attempted to be a pastor at a church in a mining community. Though my heart was there, my self-confidence and my ability to express my inner conviction, attributes that had eluded me my entire life, were still missing. In my judgement, my presentation went okay. I'm not sure what anyone heard or learned. I believed most had come to support me, and not necessarily to learn anything from me. As I alluded to earlier in this book, I was rarely a guy people came to for wisdom or counsel. And I don't blame them. In the moment, I am often at a loss for words when people do come for advice.

The bottom line is this: the Course teaches that becoming a savior of the world means changing your mind about the world—not to go out and actually "save the world" literally, even though some students are called to be formal teachers of the Course. In fact the Course even says, "Therefore, seek not to change the world, but choose to change your mind about the world." And it turns out saving the world wasn't in the cards for me, at least not in form. Though many were kind enough to buy a copy of *Enlightenment Everyone* at my launch party, the whole idea never really took off.

I believed I had been guided to write the book and create the program, and therefore believed it would be successful. I still believe I was guided to write it now, but my practice is to accept the outcome of following guidance no matter what the outcome is. In my closet downstairs right now are about three hundred copies of EE.

Today I like to think that the book will take off after I am gone, just as Vincent's art took off only after he was gone. I like to think it is the lingering self-doubts in my own mind, and not the book and concept itself, that has stalled the reading and application of *Enlightenment Everyone*. Or... the book is total crap and will never take off! I'm okay with that now. It obviously hasn't stopped me from writing. When you fall off the horse...

THIRTY-SIX

I Am With You Always

I am with you always.
—Matthew 28:20

When I said "I am with you always,"
I meant it literally. I am not absent to
anyone in any situation.
—A Course in Miracles T-7.III.1:7-8

A couple months ago (March 2021) Zeynep and I went shopping at Marshall's. After arriving we decided to split up. I went to look at shoes and art and jackets (one can never have too many jackets), while Zeynep headed off to do her thing. After awhile, I found myself idly wandering through kitchenware, when I happened upon the coffee mugs section. We have plenty of them at home, and so I had no need of one. But as I looked, one just popped out at me. On this mug it read, "I am with you always." Matthew 28:20.

A sense of light and joy shone through me after reading this mug. I had recently begun rereading the Course

Text (for the X'th time), and had *just* read this exact quote that morning! This little synchronicity, or glimpse, gave me a sense that the quote was actually true—that Jesus *is* actually with me. This teaching, that our Inner Guide—or whatever name you want to give Him or It—is *always* with us, is central to the Course, and central to the Bible for that matter, as far as I know. We are *never* alone, according to them. And so I felt a quiet happiness as I came upon this mug.

I grabbed the mug off the shelf, found Zeynep on the other side of the store, and put it in the cart. She took one look at it and rolled her eyes. We certainly don't need another coffee mug.

And after around nine years with me, she was used to me throwing all kinds of unnecessary things into the cart that have a "special" symbolic meaning to me. I pleaded, apologized, begged, said "I *have* to have it, c'mon"… she agreed reluctantly. I am drinking coffee out of it right now as I write this.

This little story brings up an important topic I have to share. *A Course in Miracles*, as well as many other authentic spiritual paths, presents many deep, seemingly complex ideas and teachings, because it is our mind which is identified with the ego that is being taught, and it believes in and values complexity. One can seem at times to get lost in all the teachings and complexities. But all that complexity and all that "spiritual striving," I have come to understand, leads to one simple, extremely simple, idea or truth: *we are not alone.*

The central experience of all of us here on earth is that we are alone—or believe we are. We are born alone. We grow up alone. We die alone. Yes, we try to join with others, through relationship (and sex), but at the end of the day, if we are honest with ourselves, we all believe we are alone. I only bring this existential stuff up because perhaps the most profound thing I have learned on my journey through this life is that I am indeed *not* alone. And no one else is either.

The understanding, and deep peace, that comes with the experience that *I am not alone* is the great gift I have learned on the spiritual journey. I shared many stories above about spiritual experiences, including the Revelation, and I believe they were all part of a greater plan to teach me that I am simply, mercifully, not alone. Ever.

This understanding and experience is the great gift that was given me. And I believe many others on a spiritual path would echo my sentiment. As the years have gone by, and I have practiced my practice (as best I can), I have slowly been able to build trust that there is indeed a Higher spiritual Presence that is within me, that is guiding me along the way. The Course calls this Presence the Holy Spirit or Jesus. Over time, I have been blessed with many signs, symbols, and synchronicities, in dreams and in my waking life, that have helped validate to me that this invisible (to my five senses) Presence is actually real, is actually there, and actually has my best interests, my happiness at heart. I, for one, can attest that what the Course and other paths teach is that I am not alone.

Little Glimpses

Here are just a couple of examples of many that have helped me learn to trust that He is actually there. In 2009, I was living in Davis and working on my first book *Enlightenment Everyone*. At this time, I had followed guidance to write the book, and really felt guided as I was writing the book. Bullwinkle the cat would lay on my desk between me and the computer as I wrote, another little Holy Spirit character helping me along the way. Anyway, as I wrote, I had been on the "spiritual journey" formally for a couple of years, and I'll be blessed if I didn't notice some unusual things happening around me.

During the time I was writing, often I would drive into busy and bustling downtown Davis. Always full of traffic, parking spots were hard to come by. You can ask my friend Chris who lives there if you don't believe me. Anyways, I noticed at this time that I was "in the flow," and that I never struggled to find a parking spot when I came into town. There was almost always a spot right where I needed one to be. I didn't even have to bother to "manifest" a parking spot, so in the flow was I, that they just came of themselves. (Really, nonbelievers, stuff like this actually happens once you start to change your mind and get on a spiritual path). I actually got used to getting a good parking spot because it was so common (I might sound like I'm boasting a bit here, and maybe I am, but there is a point to all this).

Then one day when I drove into town, I couldn't find a parking spot where I wanted. Not even close. I drove around one corner; still no spot. Then on to the next street; still, no spot. *Humph. How unusual.* I wasn't upset though. And so I thought, *I wonder what this is all about?* It was just so unusual to not find a spot.

Finally, I did find a spot a few blocks away and got out of my car and started walking. After a few blocks, headed towards my destination, I happened to walk by a local New Age-type shop, and I casually looked into the front window as I passed. And right there, displayed in the window, was a very specific spiritual book I had been looking for. "Ah!" I said. *That is why I didn't get the parking spot I wanted.* I went into the shop and bought the book.

On another occasion, I went to bed one night and had a dream. It was a lucid dream, and so I was aware I was dreaming as I dreamed. In this dream, I was walking with a young woman along the first floor of a two-story motel. We were passing by the rooms, and I was *marveling* at how *real* the building and girl seemed (because I was aware it was all a dream). Together, we headed upstairs and down the hall. We stopped at a door of one of the rooms, and I paused to reach out and touch the door. It was made out of wood, and again, I was just mesmerized at how *real* the door felt after I had reached out and touched it. I was thinking to myself, *this kinda validates the Course's teaching that the world is a dream—I can see how the mind is so powerful it can make a door so real as this.*

Anyway, the young lady and I entered the room, and there before us was a big queen bed. I'm not gonna lie. I was excited about my immediate future prospects—

I was gonna get lucky! Why not? It's only a dream, right? So we both get on the bed … and then I look to my right, and about ten feet away from the foot of the bed is a line of seven older men and women, sitting in chairs, quietly looking at me. They all had grey hair, and there was a sense of peace and wisdom about them as they looked upon us.

Believe it or not, I immediately forgot about the lovely young woman with me. I recognized at once that these older folks were Ascended Masters. I had read about others being visited by Ascended Masters in their dreams. Admittedly I had felt a little envious of them. And yet, here they were, in my dream! I got very excited, and openly and animatedly said to them, "Hey, I know you. You guys are Ascended Masters! Do you have a message for me? What is the message?" I admit, I did not act very cool here. I was like an out-of-control little boy. They did not immediately respond to me. They continued to just look at me quietly. Then I became aware that I was waking up from this dream, and worried for a moment that they wouldn't say anything. But then, just at the last instant, before I awoke, one of them said, "Meditate more." And that was it.

So I got that goin' for me, which is nice.

I still don't meditate enough.

In truth, I've had many experiences along the lines of the ones above. And I have read of many others experienced by other people. Finding the book *The Disappearance of the Universe*, the coffee mug, the little light in Mexico, Jeff showing up at just the right time, and so many other examples. These are all little glimpses, or little hints, that there is a Higher Hand guiding us along the way. Of course, there was also the Big Glimpse—the Revelation. All this in total, as I have already alluded to, is meant to get *me*, who thinks he is alone (ego) to understand and recognize that I am *not* alone (Spirit). He is with me always. And lately I have been experiencing the great peace and joy that comes with this knowledge more and more. It is the great gift of being a "spiritual" person. And I didn't even have to give up fantasy football, golf, poker, or (non-alcoholic) beer!

I have to add that also, just doing my daily spiritual practice is often enough. I read a line or two, or a paragraph, and that deep sense of peace and gratitude just returns to me. I feel His Presence then. And how blessed could I be, really?

And when I am really in what the Course calls my "right mind," I find His Presence there with me when seemingly "normal" expressions of love happen in my world: little Nonie gives me a kiss (licks) on my face and purrs in the morning, a hearty laugh from Zeynep upstairs as she talks to her sisters, a squirrel joyfully chasing her brother on the branch of a tree outside my window. On those occasions when I am in my right mind, or seeing with Spirit, the whole world becomes beautiful, an expression of Love's Presence. These are the simple, priceless gifts that come from just following.

It's not always peaches and cream

It might sound at this point like my life is all peaches and cream. That I have no troubles now, and, "Good on you, Rob! Congrats to you, dude, you must be special ..." And all that. And it is good. I cannot overstate how much inner peace has come since I have found this "spirituality" and "God" business. It just has, and that is my experience, and that is what I am sharing here. Take it or leave it.

But life on the spiritual path is not without its bumps and bruises, and it would be incomplete if I did not share at least a bit about that, too.

Being on a spiritual path, in my case a Course student, can at times be deeply painful and frustrating. I have found over the years that I am much more sensitive to any disturbing feeling or thought. A little pang of guilt or a bit of fear, experiences that would have gone virtually unnoticed in my past (before becoming "spiritual") are now felt deeply in the present. And it doesn't feel good. I've become much more sensitive. And on top of that, after having been on the path for years, it can become deeply frustrating that I do indeed still identify with the ego and have these feelings.

After awhile, it's like, "C'mon dude, when am I gonna be enlightened already?" Bad moods, guilty feelings, still afraid of what someone thinks of me, etc.... all these unpleasant manifestations of the ego continue to rise, and I am asked to keep forgiving, Course style. But after awhile, it just gets damn frustrating. In fact, just a few days ago, I simply gave up doing the Course (my practice of forgiveness) for the day. I said, "to hell with it, I'm just going to feel rotten and not do anything about it." And I did. I had a rotten day. This particular upset related to my frustration at work. I was/am getting a little tired of waking up so early at 4:50 a.m. "F this," I said! And by F, I did not mean forgive. And so I had a bad day on the path. It happens. It's part of the process of awakening, they say. So okay then.

The day after having this bad day, though, I came across a reading in the Course that reminded me that my only purpose is to heal my mind, not what I am doing here on earth. And I immediately began to feel better.

Also, briefly, for those who are not "spiritual" and not into spirituality or this "God" business at all. First, wow, you read this far. Thanks for that. Second, if you are happy with your life now, generally speaking, maybe consider holding off if you are tempted to investigate spirituality. Don't fix it if it ain't broke, so to speak. Have fun. Wait until life takes a turn and hits the fan in some way, and if/when it does, maybe then would be a good time to look into spirituality.

Third, if this book and reading has perhaps inspired you to at least begin to consider investigating spirituality, to take a first little step somewhere somehow, that is great. Go ahead. I highly encourage it. But a word of warning. If you go far enough with spirituality, it can, and probably will, turn your whole world upside down. And this "period of unsettling" can be pretty darn disturbing.

By disturbing, I don't mean just a bad day for instance, I mean it can turn one's life completely upside down—one can lose their grip on what is real and what is not. It can be extremely disorienting. So just be aware of this. This period is usually only temporary, though. After that, as I've shared in this book, there certainly *is* light at the end of the tunnel, and it is good.

The Bottom Line

The bottom line is, I still have a lot of ups and downs on the path, just as most folks do in life. It's just that there is *far* more peace and joy during the ups than there used to be. And the downs are not nearly as low as they used to be (thank God for that). While drinking spirits is okay, I have found that drinking—feeling the Presence of— Spirit is the way to a deeper, more lasting sense of ease and peace. So I'll stick with that.

THIRTY-SEVEN

Lovall Valley Road

I'M DRIVING home from the winery on Lovall Valley Road, which runs near our home in Sonoma. In the seat next to me is an empty 6.0 liter wine bottle box made of pinewood with the Gun Bun logo etched into the sides. It's a beautiful February day in 2018, with blue skies and the spring flowers getting ready to make their annual appearance.

Yet tears are welling in my eyes and I am full of emotion, for it is a heavyhearted day for me. Our mighty companion and friend of seventeen years, Bullwinkle the cat, has passed. It happened at home just this morning, and I went to the winery in order to find a makeshift coffin to bury him in. He was truly a saint of a cat, there with me through the hardest of times as well as the joyful ones. We loved Bull with all our heart and soul. And so it was a bittersweet day that we would be putting him to rest. Thankfully, his sister Nonie was still here to soften the blow. And as I write this, our miracle kitty is still with Zeynep and me.

I had been on the spiritual journey long enough to

know that what is real about "The Bull" never died. That is a silly idea. His Soul is eternal, like all living things, and all the love he is and all the love he gave will continue on into eternity. I knew all this to be true, but I still missed my friend.

And so as I was driving slowly along Lovall Valley Road back to the house, I turned to my right and happened to look up at the sky above the hill, above where our house would be. I stared in utter amazement, unable to believe what I saw. There, in the sky was a cloud, shaped just like a Jesus fish! You know—those Jesus fish you often see glued to the back of people's cars? The fish is elongated and its tail takes form as the lines cross in the back. That's what I saw in the sky.

I felt a great sense of gratitude and wonderment as I looked upon this unmistakable symbol of Christ in the sky. A symbol that my Inner Guide, Whom I choose to call Jesus, is with Bull, and still with me in this sad but lovely moment. It is a Miracle. I paused to take a couple of photos to show Zeynep. Then I took a moment in silent prayer of thanks to God for once again reminding me that I am not alone, that He is always with me, and that everything will be okay in the end.

Another wonderful little miracle involves the art that hangs in our house. After Zeynep and I were married, my mother decided to move back down to southern California, where she had grown up. She moved onto my cousin Kasey and her partner Olie's avocado farm, where she could walk her dogs freely and watch my cousin ride her beautiful prize-winning horse. Meanwhile, Zeynep and I would become renters in my mom's house.

Zeynep and I worked hard to make the house our own. We painted virtually the entire interior. We spent months shopping for the right furniture and appliances. And we had a new kitchen installed, with white quartz countertops and matching white cabinets. Yet, for the most part, we kept most of mom's beautiful art, which continues to hang on the walls.

For me, the little miracle is in the art. For her art, which I had absolutely no involvement in selecting or acquiring, seems to reflect not only mom's journey, but also my own spiritual journey as well. In our bathroom hangs a piece picturing an open door in an empty house, which I imagine is near a beach with light streaming through. The artist titled the piece *Endless Light*. That is as good description of Heaven (as I remember it) as any. In our living room is a painting of our local Sonoma Mission, where Christians had settled to spread the good news in early California history. Images of the cathedral Notre-Dame de Paris hang in our dining area. And perhaps the most striking to me is a large painting by artist Jim Waid, also in our dining area, that depicts what looks like a jungle, with swirling colors winding their way through a bleak blackness (printed in black and white on page 210).

At first sight, the painting looks dark and forbidding and chaotic. For many years, I deeply disliked this painting. It made me uncomfortable, for it seemed to reflect my own chaotic mind. But a few years ago, after I had

finally found myself on a spiritual path, I took a closer look at the painting. And lo and behold, I noticed (at last) that there is a figure standing in the middle of the painting. He is surrounded by white paint, which I see as a symbol of light surrounding his body. And he is looking at a vague horned creature which stands before him. Behind him is what appears to be a big butterfly. I couldn't help but see my own life story of forgiveness now depicted in this painting. And so this piece of art has now transformed into one of my favorite paintings in the world.

The figure surrounded by light symbolizes my safety and innocence as I stand facing the evil horned creature before me. The big butterfly behind me symbolizes the Holy Spirit, Who is now my Guide and Comforter as I continue on my journey of healing. And now identifying with the Holy Spirit, rather than the ego, for me the horned creature before me transforms from a devil-like creature into a harmless calf (the image looks somewhat like a baby cow). And so now, at last, I am at peace.

The little miracle is that all this religious and spiritual art was already in the house when Zeynep and I moved in. It is as if Spirit had gone ahead and worked through my mother to pick out the most perfect art for us for our home. Zeynep loves the art, too. We also added a couple of pieces of our own, including a beautiful watercolor of an ancient Sicilian temple painted by our lovely friend Songul. And an abstract piece I could use as a guide to describe the entire spiritual journey painted by our dear friend Kim. Our home is now a warm, comfortable abode, and Zeynep and I are grateful we get to live here for a time.

I share these stories not only because I think they are lovely stories, but because they are examples of what I have been experiencing these past few years. I can attest that so many little miracles have happened since I have been on the spiritual journey. The Jesus fish in sky was among the most striking of them, along with the inspired art collection, but I have been blessed to have experienced many others. I share this not to brag, but because I want to share what happens to those who are on the path.

After having hit the bookstores and conference circuit for so long, I've discovered countless examples of the little miracles of others who have had similar experiences to mine, and I loved every story I ever read or heard. I am so deeply grateful that I have found myself on the spiritual path, after so many bumps on the road. It's pretty freakin' cool!

Tonight, after I finish writing this and after I have dinner with Zeynep, I will go to work on Rhinefarm, out in the vineyard. I will be joining Mark, along with my cousin Towle, who is our manager and currant vineyard director and who will be providing the necessary paperwork and plan, and together Mark and I will board our brand-new orange Kubota tractors and "dust" the vineyard—spray natural sulfur dust into the vineyard to protect the vines against powdery mildew. We will start at eight p.m. and we will work deep into the wee hours of the morning (so no one will be exposed to the dust during the daytime). This is a spring farming ritual practiced all throughout wine country.

Recently, because of the coronavirus pandemic— which began a couple of months ago — my job has shifted dramatically at the winery, from tour guide (no more tourists) to tractor driver. (Note: This book was completed in 2021, and so I am back to being a tour guide once again.) As a result of the pandemic, we are farming Rhinefarm ourselves again for the first time in well over a decade, as we were forced to let go of our trusted vineyard management company who had been working Rhinefarm for us for so long. Gun Bun therefore needed workers to help farm the ranch. And so, amazingly, I'm back in the vineyard, where I haven't worked for over twenty years, since the day back in '98 when I quit the winery and marched off that hill, headed to L.A., and out into the beyond. It seems it has come full circle.

I am bouncing all over the place as my little Kubota chugs briskly between the vines at about four and a half miles per hour. If I didn't have my seatbelt on, my head would probably hit the ceiling. The rows of vines have been disked, causing big dirt clods and bumpiness, and I have to pay attention. The rows of vines are only six feet wide; too big of a bump, and I will ram the tractor into a vine or two and wipe them out. A barn owl lifts off from a grapevine into the night as the roar of my tractor approaches. Jackrabbits scamper to and fro. Field mice dash for cover. It's after one a.m., and the sky is clear and full of stars. But I can't see them through the dust-covered windshield and the sulfur dust that hangs in the air everywhere. We are protecting the vines in order that they thrive and produce the fruitful bounty, the Cabernet grapes and the Gewürztraminer grapes that will be turned into the delicious ancient beverage that has nourished people going all the way back to Jesus' time and before. And I am happy as I drive my little Kubota through all of this. My, what a difference a couple of decades make!

I can now vaguely remember farming Rhinefarm as an adolescent and young man, numb on the surface, but so full of anger underneath. Completely ego-identified, its little voice whispered that driving tractors and digging ditches was all that I was capable of doing. I had no skills or intelligence of any kind. No impulse to lead, only to follow. No ambition. Just a fruit picker am I, and nothing more.

And yet, even deeper still in my unconscious, the ego whispered madly that I was superior to tractor-driving and ditch-digging. I could start and run a great business of my own, like my grandfather Cannon had, and my dad had before me. I was more than this little job in the vineyard. And beneath all this still was my guilt, for having all these thoughts, and believing that I am separate from God, that I am self-created and on my own. Oh the guilt.

And now, today, as I whisk through the vines deep into the night in my little Kubota, virtually all of these ideas have been washed away by the Holy Spirit. No longer do I believe in striving, for thanks to the Course and Jesus, not to mention the Revelation, I have learned that my worth is not established by what I do in the world, what I say, where I go, or what I think. My worth was established by God Who created me, and so my worth is inherent, and will be with me, will be me, for the rest of eternity.

Do I still experience guilt and fear? Of course—what happens if I crash into the vines or get caught up in trellis wire, which is a hazard of driving tractors? What happens if I feel guilty for something I said to Zeynep? And sometimes I just feel afraid for no particular reason—an echo of The Plunge. But then I ask Holy Spirit to help me forgive these thoughts and fears, and before long, I am happily bouncing through the vines once again. No more do I worry about my place in the world. All that is behind me. Though I have not quite reached my ultimate goal of freedom from guilt, which is what some would call enlightenment, I can see down the road that peace of mind is on its way. Prayer for peace of mind was my first prayer all those years ago, and by my Father and through His Voice in the Course, the way has come.

It is hard to understand what
"The Kingdom of Heaven is within you"
really means...

The word "within" is unnecessary.

The Kingdom of Heaven is you.
What else **but** *you did the Creator create,*
and what else **but** *you is His Kingdom?*

—A Course in Miracles T-4.III.1:1-5

APPENDIX

What is
A Course in Miracles?

Your task is not to seek for love,
but merely to seek and find all the barriers
within yourself that you have built against it.
—ACIM T-16.IV.6:1

WHAT IS *A Course in Miracles?* There are many excellent descriptions and explanations of the Course, including in D.U. and on the website of the Course publisher, the Foundation for Inner Peace (*acim.org*). And so I will add to the list with this version:

In the original movie *Ghostbusters*, Dr. Peter Venkman (played by Bill Murray), along with the other Ghostbusters, dispose of a menacing little ghost. Afterwards, he yells, "We came, we saw, we kicked its ass!" And that, in a nutshell, is exactly what Jesus has done in this Course. Only in this case, the "little ghost" is the ego. (I'm not so sure Jesus would describe his Course that way. You'll have to forgive me!)

Yes, calm. Yes, patient. But don't be fooled. Jesus'

strength comes through as a no-nonsense, authoritative, yet loving teacher, who wants His students to succeed. Uncompromising in His approach; if you will follow where He leads, you will realize that He will ask of you to be uncompromising, too, yet patient with yourself in your practice. And in the end, you will know your Self—your True Self—which is the only one worth knowing.

In *A Course in Miracles,* Jesus has brought into our world of weariness, suffering and death a way out. The Course is a how-to manual for anyone who sincerely wishes to leave the far country—the world of fear and lack famously spoken of by Jesus 2,000 years ago in his parable of the prodigal son. After being a student of the Course for over ten years, I cannot say enough about it. To put it in highly spiritual terms, the Course is the bomb!

The Course, like all authentic spiritual paths, concerns itself with undoing the ego in the human mind, and changing the mind's perception from one of fear and guilt to one of understanding and love. This goal is accomplished in two ways. First, by guiding students through a practice of a special form of forgiveness, and second, by inspiring them to get in touch with their own Inner Teacher, which is called the Holy Spirit or Jesus. Once the student gets in touch with their Inner Teacher, she learns how to follow His guidance. In truth, it doesn't matter what you call your Inner Guide, as long as you are in touch with It, or Him, and ask Him for guidance.

That is it. Sounds simple enough. And it is. But it is certainly not easy—not for most students, and not for me.

It is a lifetime path. In fact, going through the Course as if it were a breeze means you're probably not really doing the Course. The Course can be challenging and even frustrating at times, to be sure. But it is also a lot of fun. It's a lot of fun to be learning about truth, and about your true Self, plain and simple.

What is so rare about this path is that it is a self-study course. There is no formal religion with churches to attend, unless one chooses to. No dogma. And no guru. No priest, imam, rabbi or any other external authority figure. It is just you and the Course, and hopefully, if you practice correctly, you will be introduced to your own Inner Guru, as I mentioned above.

For me, a loner type, it is the perfect course. To be sure, there are thousands of Course groups around the world which involve group meetings to study the Course, as well as several Course communities, for those who love social contact. But attending a group or joining a community is certainly not required. For instance, I studied the Course alone for over a year before I ventured to my first Course group in Davis, hosted by my friend Alexandra. When it comes down to it, it is between the student and the Voice of the Course, Who is within. And that is it.

One may ask, "Why would I want 'a way out' of the world? I love the world and would live here forever if I could." Excellent question. First, if you feel this way, you probably haven't had your *there must be another way* moment yet. You might recall at the beginning of this book I mentioned that usually people aren't attracted to or led to spirituality, particularly an authentic spiritual path, unless they have experienced some form of tragedy or suffering that effectively kicked them out of their normal everyday life. But it isn't even necessary to have a personal tragedy to recognize that the world is not all it's cracked up to be. We live on a planet of war, devastation, disease, inequity, racism, hatred and deep sadness. And that barely scratches the surface. Realization of the state of the world can bring its own pain.

In any case, once a person realizes that life is not ideal, whether it's personal or universal, then comes the time to scream to the universe: "There must be another way!" So unless and until one is capable of seeing that life is not working in some profound way, there will be no demand for change.

Second, you haven't experienced Heaven (yet). I am certain that *anyone* who's had even a small taste of Heaven would say, *To heck with this world. Get me back to perfect Love and Light ASAP!* By the way, there is another description of Heaven I didn't mention earlier, but I feel compelled to share now. The turn of phrase that often goes through my mind when I am remembering my moment in Heaven is: Orgasmic Ecstatic Bliss. That's what Heaven was like, in my experience. Yes, along with the experience of a deep fullness and profound ecstasy and bliss, Heaven also resembles a perfect sexual orgasm. Only it is far more intense. And rather than lasting a moment or two, we get that experience for the rest of eternity. Now compare that to say, a Twinkie. Which one would you rather have? Just sayin'...

Technically, the Course is a thick book that is divided into three sections: the Text, the Workbook of 365 daily Lessons, and the Manual for Teachers. The student is encouraged to study them all, of course, but not in any particular order. Rather, students may select which section of the book attracts them the most and start there. The text lays out the metaphysics of the Course, which is a fancy way of saying that the text explains just what the heck happened to get us all into this predicament of a pain- fear- and guilt-ridden world, which is where we are now. And then it tells us what to do about it.

Along with God, His Son (us—humanity), and the Holy Spirit, the text's main focus is the ego—what it is, or *seems* to be, what it does, and ultimately, how to undo it. What's complicated is the whole idea of the ego, and what it *seems* to be—because the ego does not, in reality, exist. It's complicated. I'll say more about that below.

The workbook offers 365 daily lessons intended to be practiced each day for at least a year. It is a practical application of a new thought system presented in the text. Generally, many students like to start with the workbook, because it is written in a more common everyday language, which is easier to understand. The text can be rather cryptic, at least at first, and usually takes time— sometimes a *long* time—to really understand.

The manual for teachers is for those who learn the Course to a sufficient degree, having completed both the text and the workbook, and wish to take it to the next level by becoming *teachers of God*. The one thing pointed out in the Course is that this aspect is not for everybody. Overall, the Course is comprehensive, and presents a completely new thought system, an overhaul of literally everything you have ever thought or believed about our existence on Planet Earth. For example, you might remember that my deep wish when I was younger was to perceive myself as an equal to everyone, rather than perceiving myself as below or above anybody. In our world, with its thought system based on separation, this is impossible, and seems totally illogical. How can Vlad the Impaler be equal to, say, Jesus? Or I be equal to St. Francis? Yet once the student understands the metaphysics of the Course, its explanations present us with a perfectly logical thought system that makes our inherent equality not only possible, but obvious.

From an ordinary, everyday perspective, the Course — what it is and what it teaches — is radical to the extreme. Some would say it is the most radical spiritual teaching in the world. Which is why I love it. Didn't they call Jesus a radical back in the day? The Course *definitely* fits that description, and is a perfect match for its author.

In thinking about the events of my own life with relation to finding the Course, I thought of an analogy that always gives me a little inner chuckle. From my point of view, I was given a "God proof."

During my junior year of high school, I was taking a trigonometry class. We were given proofs to solve. If memory serves, a mathematical proof is when an algebra-

ic solution, an answer to an algebraic equation, is given
to the student. The student must then work backwards in
order to arrive at the algebraic question, or equation. In
short, for me, proofs were a nightmare. Well, not really,
because I didn't do my homework very often, which is
beside the point. Proofs were rough.

And so, when thinking about me and Revelation and
the Course, I realize that I was given a God proof. The
Revelation was the *Answer*, and then my life seemed to
work on a twisted journey backwards to the *Question*,
which is: Who am I? The good news is that, unlike the
math proof, the God proof was really easy, and required
no effort at all on my part. I just lived my life, and the
proof seemed to solve itself, in the form of my journey
to *A Course in Miracles*, the finding of which helped me
understand both the question *and* the answer. In other
words, the Course has been instrumental in helping me
understand what the Revelation was, and perhaps equal-
ly important to me personally, what The Plunge was. And
all this, ultimately, helped reveal to me who, or What, I
am. The Course was, in a word, a godsend.

My favorite part about the Course, besides its valida-
tion and explanation to me of the meaning and truth behind the Revelation, is its complete and utter dismantling
of the ego. Based on all the research I've done, I don't
believe there is a spiritual document in the world that
breaks down and explains the ego better than *A Course in
Miracles*. Why is this such a big deal to me? Because, after
many years of reflection, I believe what I encountered

during The Plunge was a manifestation of the ego itself. The ego, though ironically experienced in specifics, is an abstract idea presented throughout all the spiritual teachings I have encountered, including the Course. But in The Plunge, the ego took on a specific form, which was projected in my mind. Make no mistake. Jesus pulls no punches when describing the ego in the Course. The ego is truly a ghastly piece of business, and belief in it is the cause of *all* the darkness and fear and terror in the world—war and genocide and murder and disease and abuse in every form. Here is just one sample of Jesus' descriptions of the ego:

> *The ego is insane. In fear it stands beyond the Everywhere, apart from All, in separation from the Infinite. In its insanity it thinks it has become a victor over God Himself. And in its terrible autonomy it "sees" the Will of God has been destroyed. It dreams of punishment, and trembles at the figures in its dreams; its enemies, who seek to murder it before it can ensure its safety by attacking them.* W-pII.12

In other places in the Course, Jesus describes the ego as the belief in separation. The ego is not real, in the end, but we all sure believe it is. And Jesus' Course goes about teaching us of its unreality, and the reality of God.

I call the ego a cosmic attack thought, for that is what I seemed to encounter in The Plunge. The (evil) doctor was *not* the Devil, but an outward projected image in my mind of my belief that there is a Devil. Turns out my belief was wrong. And thank God for that.

Here, mercifully, is one of the things the Course says about the Devil:

> *The mind can make the belief in separation very real and very fearful, and this belief is the devil. It is powerful, active, destructive, and clearly in opposition to God, because it literally denies His Fatherhood. Look at your life and see what the devil has made. But realize that this making will surely dissolve in the light of truth, because its foundation is a lie.* ACIM T-3.VII.5:1-4

And now, on to lighter pastures …

When the Course is not talking about the ego, or what we are *not*, it is spending most of its time trying to teach us what we are. In other words, it attempts to help us, its students, achieve the eons-old mystical admonition: *Know thyself.* Don't take this personally, dear reader, but if you are like me and 99.9% of the rest of the global population, you don't have a clue who or what you are. It's just the way it is. You think you're John Doe or Jane Smith, or in my case, Rob Bundschu. But in all three cases, we are dead wrong.

But if we are not who we think we are, then who are we? That *is* the question—the one all authentic spiritual paths, including the Course, attempt to answer.

Christ Spirit, created of Love and Light, *in* Love and Light, by God. That is what we are. (I dropped the mic.)

Okay. So I can say that. And it is true. We are not our

bodies, which are separate, temporary and vulnerable. We are Spirit, which is whole, eternal, and completely invulnerable to anything that happens to us here on earth (in our bodies). As Spirit, we can sleep, but we *cannot* die. We are eternal.

I can say this. But will it have any meaning to most people? No. It will not. To know truth, or to know ourselves, we can't talk about it or draw it up on a chalkboard. We have to experience it for ourselves. It's like the movie *The Matrix*—an awesome spiritual movie—in which Morpheus tells Neo, "Unfortunately, no one can be told what the Matrix is. You have to experience it for yourself."

So it is with spirituality. I could write for days about our being love and light and Spirit, as *so* many others already have, but it will be only so helpful, in the end. Because words are, as the Course teaches, merely symbols of symbols, twice removed from reality. You have to *experience* truth for yourself. This is the way.

That is what the Course, and all authentic spiritual paths, are for. To help their students or adepts *experience for themselves* what they are, from *within*. Only then can you begin to change your beliefs about yourself. Only then will you begin to get a glimmer of your Self, the famous Self everyone is ultimately looking for—even if they are not aware of it. In fact, everyone is on the journey of *Know thy self*, even if many are wholly unaware of it. The Course is a way to Know thy Self. Practice enough with it, and eventually the student will begin to get that direct experience.

Around '07 or '08, when I was living in Davis and beginning with the Course, one day I wrote a list of one hundred things I wanted, like to learn French and eat better. It was a total stream-of-consciousness thing. Item number ten on the list was, "Learn to love everyone unconditionally." That little goal was right in there with publish a book and exercise more. I didn't understand that I already had at my disposal the means to achieve this seemingly impossible goal —the Course. How can anyone ever love *everyone* unconditionally, with *so* many bastards and bastardettes out there!?

In short, the Course presents an entirely new thought system that I've mentioned above, one that completely changes a person's perception of the world and people and, ultimately, themselves. With this new thought system, a Course student learns to look on the same world as everyone else, but the meaning of everything and everyone perceived is completely changed. In this shift, a way is given to see every single human being, no matter how good or how evil they might seem, as the same: innocent. If a student can perceive everyone, including themselves, as innocent, rather than guilty and sinful, then it makes sense that they can love them. The question then is, how in the heck can you see everyone as innocent, with so many of the aforementioned guilty bastard and bastardettes out there?

The Course answers that with perfect logic. It goes back to the beginning. Remember the famous "fall" of Adam and Eve from the Garden? When God kicked them out of there for sinning like there's no tomorrow? This supposed historic act has meant that now we, as *sinners*, millions of years later, have to jump through a lot of religious hoops to get back into Heaven! Well, guess what? It never happened. There was no "fall."

The Course uses the term "separation" rather than "fall." There was no separation from God. Never happened, never will, no sir. Jesus reminds us in the Course, as he was reminding folks 2,000 years ago, that *there was no fall or separation*. We only *believe* there was. And *that* is our only real problem, which has been covered over since by all the millions of other problems in the world. We all remain as God created us. Right now. We are all One with Him—*now*. There was no "Original Sin." There is no sin. We are Spirit. *Now*. And forever. It only *appears* that we are something else, namely our sinful bodies and personalities.

How is it there is no sin, given all the human attacks and viciousness we have seen and experienced throughout history, both outside us and within us? This makes sense, or is perfectly logical, only if the Course student is willing to accept the central lesson the Course attempts to teach: that the world is a dream. One of its core teachings is that the world, and everybody in it, is not real, but an illusion. This idea may startle many readers. It is the "radical to the extreme" idea in the Course, to be sure. But if you made it this far, I figured I might as well lay it on you.

The idea that the world is an illusion is not new, in

fact, but goes back to antiquity. In the East, many mystics call the world *maya*, which means magic or illusion. In short, gurus from across the world for millennia have been teaching their students that the world is a dream, or illusion, among other things. It's just not taught commonly in the mainstream media or universities.

Anyway, hearing this radical idea won't have much meaning, unless a person actually *experiences* this idea that the world is a dream. And that is what the Course, as well as all authentic spiritual paths, are for: to learn of the purely nondualistic truth that *only* God is real, and *nothing else* is real.

And so as it turns out, my grandmother Mary, with her three little monkeys, was right all along! To put it in terms she may have been proud of: Hear no evil, See no evil, Speak no evil, *because there is no evil*—it's all just a dream.

Naturally, hiking around Judea 2,000 years ago, telling people there is no sin, at a time when people were randomly nailed to crosses along the road, got Jesus into hot water. I imagine if anyone besides my mother reads this book, I may get into hot water, too, for saying the same thing. Anyway, saying there is no sin in humanity (the opposite of what many religions teach, including Christianity), after looking around this crazy world of ours, is quite the radical idea. As I said, the Course is radical.

Back to the movies. In another awesome film, *Inception*, starring Leonardo DiCaprio and Elliot Page, Leo's character Dom Cobb is tasked with planting an idea into someone's subconscious mind. With that idea implanted, the ideas of this person's whole outlook and belief about himself and the world will shift.

In the same way, Jesus, by means of the Course, attempts to plant an idea into students' minds—an idea that is already there, actually—that will hopefully grow into a perfect white Lily of Innocence. The Course presents its students with an idea called the Atonement, and it is this idea that Jesus is attempting—through the Course—to "plant" in our minds. Pretty freaking cool! What Jesus explains is that the Atonement is actually at the very center of our mind, deep, deep in the subconscious, below the level where the unconscious ideas of sin and guilt reside.

I remember when I encountered the idea of Atonement in the Course for the very first time. It appears in the first pages of the book, and when I read about it I had absolutely no idea what in good heavens the author was talking about. The Atonement was an enigma wrapped in a riddle tied together with a conundrum. Eventually I had to read the Course at least a couple of times, along with *Disappearance of the Universe* and some of Ken Wapnick's work, to finally get a handle on what the Atonement means. I may not do it justice, but I'll try.

In short, the Atonement is God's Answer to our *seeming* fall or separation. It has nothing to do with Christianity's teachings of sacrifice. In effect, the idea of the Atonement is the total opposite of the currently accepted ideas regarding our collective human experience.

Today, most of us believe we are separate and alone on the inside, an island unto ourselves. We each have our own will and private thoughts. Essentially, we are the authors of our own lives. God seems to have nothing to do with our everyday life, or the world, for that matter. This sense of separation and aloneness is the thought system of the ego, and the ego is the teacher we all identify with.

The idea of Atonement, on the other hand, teaches that though we may seem to be on our own, way down deep in our unconscious mind, we in truth are *not* separate and we are *not* on our own. The Holy Spirit, or Light, is in the center of our unconscious mind, and it is Spirit that transcends the world and is at One with the Holy Spirit of God, Who is real and is everywhere. We, then, all literally have a direct relationship with God Himself, though many of us are not aware of it, and don't even want it. (Why we would not want a relationship with God is another story. This the reader can learn about if the Course holds any appeal to her or him. In the Course, you will gain a clearer idea of the ego and its part in the non-existent, never-happened separation from God, as well.)

Hence, you could break down the word Atonement to be at-One-ment. We are all One with each other and God *now*. And this is the truth, no matter who we are, where we live, or what we believe. Thus, teaching that the Atonement, and not separation, is the truth, is the goal of the Course. This is true as well of other authentic spiritual paths, though the other paths would use different language and concepts to teach the same thing.

There is another practice the Course emphasizes over and over that I have had a very difficult time (of late) practicing. That is, asking for guidance. What the practice of the Course ultimately leads to is the realization that we are not alone. There is a real Spiritual Presence, which the Course calls the Holy Spirit, which is really there and waiting for us to get out of our own way and ask Him for guidance. Doing this consistently takes some serious change of habits and practice. We are secretly afraid to ask for guidance because we believe the guidance will be something we don't want to hear, or do, or be.

Anyway, over the years, I have asked for guidance a lot, even long before I ever knew about the existence of the Course. In fact, many do ask for and follow guidance, though they would never think of it that way. They simply make choices, or say or do things based on an intuitive feeling, and that intuitive feeling is often the Spirit's guidance. Yet the act of asking acknowledges that I *don't know*. One must get over the feeling of inadequacy that *don't know* implies, and then the door opens for a deeper solution to emerge.

Asking *is* a big part of the Course. Lately, I have noticed that for the most part I have not been asking consistently, for whatever reason. And so my experience of peace has also not been consistent. I'll change that, and will ask Holy Spirit now what to do. My guidance tells me that I should start to wrap up my description of the Course, lest those readers not too interested in it begin to fall into a coma.

I cannot share what I have learned from *A Course in Miracles* without mentioning its main practice: forgiveness. Reading and understanding the concepts in the Course text is not enough. Doing the workbook is important, but not enough. One *must* practice forgiveness if they wish to reach the goal of the Course, which is complete freedom from the ego (a *deeply* happy place to be). The practice called *forgiveness* has no resemblance at all to what most people think of when they think about forgiving.

The usual pattern goes something like this: Someone wrongs you in some way. It might be as simple as an unkind or cutting remark which wounded you. Or it could be something a lot worse, like someone betraying your trust, or damaging something of yours.

Now the usual form of forgiveness is, "I forgive you. But don't let this happen again, or else!" The "forgiver" sees sin first, *then* tries to overlook it. Effectively, we are saying, "You are bad and thoughtless (sinful), but I'm going to be the bigger person in this situation and overlook what you did to me because I am so special and, let's face it, above you." In effect, then, we look down on the one we are "forgiving." And they are never really freed from their sense of guilt.

This type of forgiveness, so common in the world, is ego-based. It has nothing to do with actually letting go of the offense. Usually the result is a combination of several submerged, suppressed negative emotions, like rage or resentment. Is this really loving? We are making the forgiven one *guilty as charged*, even as we say we are forgiving them. This type of forgiveness—what the Course calls "forgiveness to destroy"—is not what the Course is teaching.

The Course's form of forgiveness is entirely different, which is why it is a lifelong practice and path for most of its students. It takes a long time to truly learn to forgive our brothers and ourselves as the Course teaches. The Course teaches the forgiver to see no sin in the first place! Because, remember, only our True Self, Christ, is real, and *nothing else* is real (including our bodies and whatever error seemed to occur to our body or that of a loved one).

Spirit, our True Self, is invulnerable and eternal. So no matter the "transgression,"—even if it is atrocious, to Spirit there was no sin, because only Spirit is real, and nothing else is real, and Spirit cannot be harmed. Nothing can harm Spirit, so there is never any sin that can be committed against it, because no act can affect it. Your words, your actions, cannot harm me; I am Spirit. My words, my actions, cannot harm you; You are Spirit. Hence, there is no guilt. The moment we accept ourselves as anything less, we allow for guilt and harm and shame and—ultimately—condemnation in the form of "forgiveness."

So let us consider a "wrong" that has been done to you. Perhaps someone damages something you value, like your car. That person may initially be guilty of a crime in your judgement and deserves your anger and possibly punishment. But then you stop and drop this story in your mind and choose to forgive, Course style, instead. You first *ask* the Holy Spirit to help you look at this situation differently. And He gives you right-minded ideas (forgiving ideas), like: "But in fact, what happened? Nothing. Something *seemed* to get damaged, or dented. But it is not real (remember, the world is a dream). This is *not* a sin. There is no sin. Because the car is not ultimately real, but the Spirit in your brother, that *is* your brother, *is*."

And so, if you can let go of the "I've been done wrong" belief, you realize that nothing really has happened. There is no damage, because *only* the perfect Spirit within both you *and* the "offender" is real, and nothing else about either the "transgressor" or you, the "victim" is real. And so all is forgiven. The children of God are *innocent.*

Let us consider another example. Something happens that creates a great rift. Harsh words, or behavior that seems unforgivable (like adultery). It does not seem easy then to say, "I forgive you. Nothing happened. It's only a dream." Instead, thoughts like "I know you didn't intend harm, but I am really pissed off about this" constantly roil around in your mind, going over and over the incident. And in the end, you feel really awful, angry, resentful, hurt. *How* can you just let this go and forgive it?

The answer is that you engage in your forgiveness practice (taught in the Course), again. And again. It is a practice. And it takes much practice. You use your forgiveness practice to remind yourself that it is the ego that holds on to anger, hurt, accusation, blame and guilt, but *you* do not. And this ego reaction is harmful not only to the transgressor, but to you. When you recognize this, and, choosing instead to switch over to the Holy Spirit's perception or interpretation, decide to see the situation differently, you are released from the ego's hold on you. You then overlook the person or situation, and see only innocence. The relief can be remarkable. You are no longer tied to the ego's dark way of looking at things. You can now release not only yourself, but the person who committed the error. There is no more resentment or anger, only calm understanding.

Course forgiveness, then, is a practice where the student learns to *overlook* whatever "sin" or "crime" someone committed, see it as illusion, and instead focus all of their mind and attention on the original innocence and Spirit and light at the center of the "sinner's" being, and remember *that* only.

Students are asked to remind themselves that their brother is truly eternal light, created perfect by God, innocent, and therefore unable to really hurt or damage anyone, including you. Whatever crime our brother has committed is perceived by the Course student as illusion, or not real. Only love and light is real, and everything else is illusion.

Forgiveness is recognizing that you, too, are Spirit, love and light. You *cannot* be harmed nor do harm; you and your sister are invulnerable. Forgiveness is also recognizing that we, ourselves, believe we have committed sins, and hold guilt within us. When we learn to forgive another's "transgression"—whatever that might be—

in the process we are also forgiving ourselves. We give the gift of forgiveness to ourselves whenever we truly forgive another.

Using this superpower X(Christ)-ray vision (to gently overlook illusions and see divine innocence in *everyone*) can and does bring a great sense of inner peace and joy that comes not from this world, but another world beyond. That is what the Course is for, to practice making that correction, or shift, in the mind. That is what the Course calls the Miracle.

It is certainly not easy to practice the Course's kind of forgiveness. Often one has to forgive a transgression over and over again. Sometimes it can take years to finally forgive a person. But it *is* possible. And the inner peace that comes with it is a peace that is out of this world.

Forgiveness to overlook—seeing every One as innocent and holy, underneath whatever "sin" their body committed—is the way of the Course. Some might argue this is a form of denial. And they are right! It is a practice of denying what is false in favor of what is true.

The practice of forgiveness is taught in much greater detail in the Course and D.U., of course. But this brief synopsis will hopefully give you an idea of what the Course is actually saying. We are holy eternal beings, *not* sinners trapped in time. We are one with God and with each other, forever and forever. And I was blessed to experience this fact directly in the Revelation. So now I seek to forgive others and *myself*, so I can remember who I am. Amen.

The last thing I'd like to mention about the Course is the Course's take on going to Heaven. It teaches that Heaven is not attained through death, but by awakening. Religions around the world have taught that a person must jump through a bunch of religious hoops—rituals, acceptance of doctrines, sacrifice, etc., during their life, and then when they die, they get to go to Heaven—while everyone else burns! Ah, no. That is not the way it goes.

In order to return from the far country (our world) to Heaven, one must awaken to who they really are (*Know thy Self*), simply (but not easily) by doing the necessary inner work. In short, you must prepare your mind, make it ready for all that love and light and bliss in Heaven. One cannot enter Heaven unless she is like Heaven. Thus the mind cannot enter Heaven with *any* darkness, or any fear or guilt-based emotion, thought, or belief. The mind in effect must be completely purified of all that dark gobbledygook still buried in the unconscious mind.

In order to purify the mind, then, one must go inward and bring up all that dark stuff from the unconscious to the conscious mind, then look at it *with Spirit*, see that it is harmless, and finally let it go. This is the process of undoing the ego. Amazingly, most of us are addicted to our guilt and fear because they are necessary in order to maintain our separate personal identity, and so we have no desire to let them go. That is why the majority of people are not on an authentic spiritual path. And it is why practicing forgiveness is the Course's way of getting the job done. Other authentic spiritual paths will use other methods that can lead to the same result.

Once *all* that guilt and fear in the unconscious mind is finally released, what is left is one's healed whole mind, or true mind, which is perfect love and light and all that is good. One will be awake. Then, shortly thereafter, according to the Course, God Himself will come down and lift you back up to Heaven, where you will discover that you never left. Amen.

EPILOGUE

And on one final note, I'm happy to say that getting lit was the way to happiness after all. I just had to figure out Who to get lit with:

God has lit your mind Himself, and keeps your mind lit by His light because His light is what your mind is. This is totally beyond question, and when you question it you are answered. The Answer merely undoes the question by establishing the fact that to question reality is to question meaninglessly. That is why the Holy Spirit never questions. His sole function is to undo the questionable and thus lead to certainty. The certain are perfectly calm, because they are not in doubt. They do not raise questions, because nothing questionable enters their minds. This holds them in perfect serenity, because this is what they share, knowing what they are.
—ACIM T-7.III.5:1-8

Beyond the body, beyond the sun and stars, past
everything you see and yet somehow familiar, is an arc
of golden light that stretches as you look into a great and
shining circle. And all the circle fills with light before your
eyes. The edges of the circle disappear, and what is in it is no
longer contained at all. The light expands and covers every-
thing, extending to infinity forever shining and with no break
or limit anywhere. Within it everything is joined in perfect
continuity. Nor is it possible to imagine that anything could
be outside, for there is nowhere that this light is not.

—Jesus, ACIM T-21.I.8:1-6

ACKNOWLEDGMENTS

I wish to express my heartfelt thanks to the following people and organizations who made this book, and my life story, possible.

First, many thanks to the late Davina Rubin, my first developmental editor whose inestimable insights and work helped make this book actually readable, and hopefully enjoyable as well. May you be dancing with the Angels for the rest of eternity. To Valerie Valentine, whose copy editing, proofreading, and recommendations helped fill in some gaps and generally put the final touches on the final version. Your insightful observations and warm encouragement were truly helpful and deeply appreciated. And finally, to my fearless friend and mentor, D. Patrick Miller, thank you for putting your years of experience and knowledge in the writing and publishing world into the production of this book, for your kind and poignant remarks in the Foreword, and your never-ending gentle laughter through it all. I'm more than happy and honored to be your mainline source of Pinot Noir!

Next, my deep thanks and appreciation to my family and all my friends, who have encouraged me, been infinitely patient and forgiving, and stuck with me through thick and thin over the years. Believe me, there was a lot of "thin" to go along with the "thick." And since many of you are named in this book, thank you in advance for letting me include you in my life's story. It simply wouldn't be the same without you.

To all my coworkers past and present at Gun Bun, you rock! Thank you for making the many hours of my daily journey enjoyable and full of fun (or at least as much fun as we can have on the clock!). A toast to you.

To all the community of *A Course in Miracles* including FIP, FACIM, Rev. Tony Ponticello and his Conference holders, authors, teachers and fellow students, (is this sounding like an Oscars® speech yet!?), thank you for your Good Work, in helping me heal my mind and bringing great joy into my life. You guys and gals are the best!

And finally, to my lovely wife Zeynep for being there as a source of strength, support, encouragement, and infinite patience through the two-plus years I have been plugging away on this project, my thanks and love for you is forever. This work—and my world—would not be what it is without your grace and lovely presence in my life. Love you always, askim.

CPSIA information can be obtained
at www.ICGtesting.com
Printed in the USA
FSHW021323250122
87908FS

9 780990 975045